Date Due

ON EVERYTHING

ON EVERYTHING

BY

HILAIRE BELLOC

Essay Index Reprint Series

BOOKS FOR LIBRARIES PRESS

FREEPORT, NEW YORK

First Published 1910
Reprinted 1970

INTERNATIONAL STANDARD BOOK NUMBER:
0-8369-1865-7

LIBRARY OF CONGRESS CATALOG CARD NUMBER:
70-128208

PRINTED IN THE UNITED STATES OF AMERICA

CONTENTS

	PAGE
ON SONG	1
ON AN EMPTY HOUSE	7
THE LANDFALL	16
THE LITTLE OLD MAN	22
THE LONG MARCH	29
ON SATURNALIA	38
A LITTLE CONVERSATION IN HEREFORDSHIRE .	45
ON THE RIGHTS OF PROPERTY . . .	53
THE ECONOMIST	60
A LITTLE CONVERSATION IN CARTHAGE . .	68
THE STRANGE COMPANION	74
THE VISITOR	81
A RECONSTRUCTION OF THE PAST . . .	90
THE REASONABLE PRESS	97
ASMODEUS	104
THE DEATH OF THE COMIC AUTHOR . .	113
ON CERTAIN MANNERS AND CUSTOMS . .	121
THE STATESMAN	130
THE DUEL	138

On Everything

PAGE

On a Battle, or "Journalism," or "Points of View" 148

A Descendant of William Shakespeare . . 159

On the Approach to Western England . . 167

The Weald 174

On London and the Houses in It . . . 180

On Old Towns 187

A Crossing of the Hills 194

The Barber 201

On High Places 209

On Some Little Horses 217

On Streams and Rivers 223

On Two Manuals 230

On Fantastic Books 238

The Unfortunate Man 244

The Contented Man 253

The Missioner 261

The Dream 270

The Silence of the Battlefields . . . 276

Novissima Hora 283

On Rest 289

ON EVERYTHING

ON EVERYTHING

On Song   ∽   ∽   ∽   ∽   ∽

S OME say that when that box was opened wherein lay ready the evils of the world (and a woman
opened it) Hope flew out at last.

That is a Pagan thing to say and a hopeless one,
for the true comfort that remained for men, and that
embodied and gave reality to their conquering struggle against every despair, was surely Song.

If you would ask what society is imperilled of
death, go to one in which song is extinguished.
If you would ask in what society a permanent sick-
ness oppresses all, and the wealthy alone are permitted to make the laws, go to one in which song
is a fine art and treated with criticism and used
charily, and ceases to be a human thing. But if
you would discover where men are men, take for
your test whether songs are always and loudly sung.

Sailors sing. They have a song for work and
songs for every part of their work, and they have
songs of reminiscence and of tragedy, and many
farcical songs; some brutal songs, songs of repose,

and songs in which is packed the desire for a distant home.

Soldiers also sing, at least in those Armies where soldiers are still soldiers. And the Line, which is the core and body of any army, is the most singing of them all. The Cavalry hardly sing, at least until they get indoors, for it would be a bumping sort of singing, and gunners cannot sing for noise, while the drivers are busy riding and leading as well. But the Line sings; and if you will consider quickly, all the great armies of the world, and consider them justly, not as the pedants do, but as men do who really feel the past, you would hear mounting from them always continual song. Those men who marched behind Cæsar in his triumph sang a song, and the words of it still remain (so I am told); the armies of Louis XIV and of Napoleon, of the Republic, and even of Algiers, made songs of their own which have passed into the great treasury of European letters. And though it is difficult to believe it, it is true, the little troops of the Parliament marching down the river made a song about Mother Bunch, coupled with the name of the Dorchester Hills; but I may be wrong. I was told it by a friend; he may have been a false friend.

They sang in the Barons' wars; they sang on the way to Lewes. They sang in that march which led men to the assault at Hastings, for it was written by those who saw the column of knights advancing to the foot of the hill that Taillefer was chosen for

his great voice and rode before the host, tossing his
sword into the air and catching it again by the hilt
(a difficult thing to do), and singing of Charlemagne
and of the vassals who had died under Roncesvalles.

Song also illuminates and strengthens and vivifies
all common life, and on this account what is left of
our peasantry have harvest songs, and there are
songs for mowing and songs for the mid-winter rest,
and there is even a song in the south of England
for the gathering of honey, which song, if you have
not heard it, though it is commonly known, runs
thus :—

Bees of bees of Paradise,
Do the work of Jesus Christ,
Do the work which no man can.
God made man, and man made money,
God made bees and bees made honey.
God made big men to plough, to reap, and to sow,
God made little boys to keep off the rook and the crow.

This song is sung for pleasure, and, by the way of
singing it, it is made to scan.

Indeed, all men sing at their labour, or would so
sing did not dead convention forbid them. You will
say there are exceptions, as lawyers, usurers, and
others; but there are no exceptions to this rule
where all the man is working and is working well,
and is producing and is not ashamed.

Rowers sing, and their song is called a Barcarolle;
and even men holding the tiller who have nothing
to do but hold it tend to sing a song. And I will

On Everything

swear to this that I have heard stokers when they were hard pressed starting a sort of crooning chorus together, which shows that there is hope for us all.

The great Poets who are chiefly this, men capable of perfect expression (though of no more feeling than any other of their kind), are dignified by Song, much more than by any others of their forms of power. Consider that song of Du Bellay's which he translated out of the Italian, and in which he has the winnower singing as he turns the winnowing fan. That is great expression, because no man can read it without feeling that if ever he had to do the hard work of winnowing this is the song he would like to sing.

Song also is the mistress of memory, and though a scent is more powerful, a song is more general, as an instrument for the resurrection of lost things Thus exiles who of all men on earth suffer most deeply, most permanently, and most fruitfully, are great makers of songs. The chief character in songs —that almost any man can write them, that any man at all can sing them, and that the greatest are anonymous—is never better proved than in this quality of the songs of exiles. There is a Highland song of which I have been told, written in the Celtic dialect and translated again into English by I know not whom, which, for all its unknown authorship (and I believe its authorship to be unknown) enshrines that radiantly beautiful line :

And we in dreams behold the Hebrides.

On Song

The last anonymous piece of silver that was struck
in the mint of the Roman language has that same
poignant quality.

> Exul quid vis canere?

All the songs that men make (and they are powerful
ones) regretting youth are songs of exile, and in a
sense (it is a high and true sense) the mighty hymns
are songs of exile also.

> Qui vitam sine termino
> Nobis donet in patria,

that is the pure note of exile, and so is the

> Coheredes et sodales
> In terra viventium,

and in this last glorious thing comes in the note of
marching and of soldiers as well as the note of
separation and of longing.   But after all the mention
of religion is in itself a proof of song, for what spell
could there ever be without incantation, or what
ritual could lack its chaunt?

If any man wonders why these two, Religion and
Song, are connected, or thinks it impious that they
should so be, let him do this: if he is an old man let
him cover his face with his hand and remember at
evening what occasions stand out of the long past
full of a complete life, and of an acute observation
and intelligence of all that was around: how many
were occasions for song !   There are pictures a man
will remember all his life only because he watched

them for a pastime, because he heard a woman singing as he watched them, and there are landscapes
which remain in the mind long after other things have
faded, but so remain because one went at morning with
other men along the road singing a walking song.
And if it is a young man who wishes to make trial of
this truth, he also has his test. For he will note as
the years continue how, while all other pleasures
lose their value and gradation, Song remains, until
at last the notes of singing become like a sort of
sacrament outside time, not subject to decay, but
always nourishing men, for Song gives a permanent
sense of futurity and a permanent sense of the presence of Divine things. Nor is there any pleasure
which you will take away from middle age and leave
it more lonely, than this pleasure of hearing Song.

It is that immortal quality in the business which
makes it of a different kind from the other efforts of
men. Write a good song and the tune leaps up to
meet it out of nothingness. It clothes itself with
tune, and once so clothed it continues on through
generations, eternally young, always smiling, and
always ready with strong hands for mankind. On
this account every man who has written a song can
be certain that he has done good; any man who has
continually sung them can be certain that he has
lived and has communicated life to others.

It is the best of all trades, to make songs, and the
second best to sing them.

On an Empty House ∾   ∾   ∾   ∾

A MAN a little over forty years of age had desired to take a house in London. He had lived hitherto between a cottage in the country, where he had stables and where he made it his pleasure to ride, and rooms in town off St. James's Street. He had also two clubs, one of which he continually visited. From his thirtieth year onward he had come more often to town; he was heavier in build; he rode with less pleasure. He had taken to writing and had published more than one little study, chiefly upon the creative work of other men. He was under no compulsion to write or to do any other thing, for he had a private fortune of about £3000 a year. This he managed with some ability so that it neither increased nor diminished, and like many other Englishmen, he had wisely invested abroad, from the year 1897 onwards. Now, I say, that middle age was upon him, London controlled him more and more. He was in sympathy with the maturity of the great town, which responded to his own maturity. He could find a leisure in it which he had never found in youth. The multitude of the books and the easy access to them, the sensible and varied conversation of men of his own rank and age, and that sort of

7

peopled quiet which supports the nights of men
living in London—all these had become a sort of food
to him; they greatly pleased him. So also did the
physical food of London. He took an increasing
pleasure in changing the choice of his wine, which
(an invariable effect of age) he now distinguished.
His rooms in London had thus become for now some
years past more and more his home; but he had
begun to feel that rooms could not be a home; and
he would set up for himself; he would be a master.
He would feel again and in a greater way that comfortable consciousness of self and of surroundings
fitting one which a man has in early youth every
time he enters his father's house.

With this purpose the man of whom I speak
looked at several houses, going first to agents, but
finding himself disappointed in all. He soon learned
a wiser way, which was to ask friends of what houses
they had heard, and then to see for himself whether
he liked them, and to do this before even he knew
what rent was asked. Also he would wander up and
down the streets, his heavy, well-dressed figure pon-
derous and moving at a measured pace, and as he so
wandered he would cast his eyes over houses.

London, like all great things, has about it a quality
for which I do not know the word, but when I was
at school there was a Greek word for it. "Mani-
fold" is too vague; "multitudinous" would not explain the idea at all. What I mean is a quality by
which one thing contains several (not many) parts,

8

each individual, each with a separate life and colour of its own, and yet each living by a common spirit which builds up the whole. Thus London, a great town, is also a number (not a large number) of towns within. And to this man, who had cultivation and so often wrote upon the creative work of other men, the spirit and the delight of each quarter was well known. The words "Chelsea," "Soho," "Mayfair," "Westminster," "Bloomsbury"—all meant to him things as actual as colours or as chords of music, and each represented to him not measurable advantages or drawbacks, but separate kinds of pleasure. He loved them all, but he gravitated, as it is right and natural that a man of his wealth and sort should do, to the houses north of Oxford Street and south of the Marylebone Road. He had no territorial blood, nor had his ancestry engaged in commerce; he was European in every ramification of his descent. He came of doctors, of soldiers, of lawyers, and in a word, of that middle class which has now disappeared as a body and remains among us only in a few examples whose tradition, though we respect it, is no longer a corporate tradition. For three hundred years his people had had Greek, Latin, and French, and had in alternate generations experienced ease or constraint according to the circumstances of English life. He was the first to enjoy so complete a leisure.

To this part of London, therefore, he naturally turned at last, and following the sound rule that

a man's rent should be one-tenth of his income—
if that income is moderate—he looked about for
a large and comfortable house. The very streets had
separate atmospheres for him. He fixed at last upor
what seemed a very nice house indeed in Queen
Anne Street. First he looked at it well from without, admired the ironwork and the old places for
lanterns, and the extinguishers; he looked at the
solid brick, and at that expression which all houses
have from the position of their windows. It was a
house such as his own people might have built or
lived in under George III, and in the earlier part
of the reign of that unfortunate, though virtuous,
monarch. In a little while he had gone so far as to
get his ticket from the agent, and he would view the
house. He came one day and another; he was very
much taken with the arrangement of it and with the
quiet rooms at the back, and he was pleased to see
that the second staircase was so arranged that there
would be little noise of service. He remembered
with a sort of sentimental but pleasing feeling his
childhood passed in such a house, for his father had
been a surgeon, somewhat famous, and they lived in
such rooms and in such a neighbourhood. He was
pleased with the old-fashioned arrangements for
heating the water; he did not propose to change
them. But he was glad that electric light had taken
the place of gas, and he did propose to change the
disposition of this light made by the last tenants.

With every day that he visited the place it pleased

him more. It became a daily occupation of his, and
it took up most of his thoughts. The agents were
gentle and kind ; no mention of competitors was
made, and the reason for this would have been plain
to any other but himself, for he was offering a larger
rent than the house was worth. But his offer was
not yet confirmed. Many years of successful investment, in which, as I have said, he had neither increased nor diminished his fortune, had given him a
just measure of prudence in these affairs, and he
would not sign in a definite way until the whole
scheme was quite clear in his mind. For a week he
visited and revisited, until the caretaker, an elderly
woman of rich humour, began to count upon the
conversation which she enjoyed at his daily appear-
ances.

. . . . . .

In the wealthier part of London—next door to
the modern abomination of some new man or other
who was destined to no succession, to no honour,
and whose fate in the future would probably prove
to be some gamble or other upon the Continent—
next door to such a house, just round the corner, so
that you could only see the Park sideways, lived an
admirable woman. She was the wife of a Peer and
the mother of numerous children, of whom the
eldest now served as a soldier and was an expense
to them, as was the youngest, from the traditions of
his school, which was also expensive. It was her

husband's business, when that half of the politicians
to which he belonged was not in office, to speak at
meetings and to write lithographed letters im-
ploring aid of the financial kind for institutions
designed to relieve the necessities of the poor. He
also shot both on his own land and on that of
friends, and he would fish in Scotland, but as he
had no land there, he had to hire the fishing. The
same was true of his sport with the birds in that
Northern Kingdom; so one way and another they
were not rich for their position, and this admirable
woman it was who made all things go well. She
was strong in body, handsome in face, and of a
clear, vivacious temper, which pleased all the world
about her, and made it the better for her presence.
But none of these attributes were so worthy, nor
gave her so general an admiration, as the splendid
and evident virtue of her soul. There was in her
very gesture, and in every tone of her voice when
she chose to be serious, that fundamental character
of goodness which is at once the chief gift to
mortals from Almighty God, and the chief glory
and merit of those recipients who have used it well.
She had done so, and the whole of her life was a
sacrament and a support to all who were blessed
with her acquaintance.

Among these was the Man who was taking the
House, for he had known her brother very well at
college. She was much of the same rank as himself, though a little older. During many years of

On an Empty House

his youth he had so taken for granted her perfections and her companionship, that these had, as it were, made his world for him; he had judged the world by that standard. Now that he knew the world, he used that standard no more. It would not be just to say that at her early marriage he had felt any pain save a necessary loss of some companionship. He had never had a sister; he continued to receive her advice and to enter her house as a relative, for though he was not a relative, the very children would have been startled had they ever chosen to remember that he was not one, and his Christian name came as commonly upon their lips, upon hers, and upon her husband's as any name under their own roof. He would not, of course, finally take this house until she had seen it.

He was waiting, therefore, in the hall one morning of that winter a little impatiently to show her his choice, and to take her verdict upon certain details of it before he should write the last letter which should bind him to the place. He heard a motor-car come up, looked out and saw that it was hers, and met her upon the steps and led her in. She also was pleased with everything she saw, and her pleasure suddenly put light into the house, so that if you had seen her there, moving and speaking and laughing, you would have had an illusion that the sun had come shining in all the windows; a true physical illusion. You would have remembered the place as sunlit. She noted the panelling, she

13

approved of one carved fireplace, she disapproved of
another; she said the house was too large for him;
she was sure it would suit him. She showed him
where his many books would go, and warned him
on a hundred little things which he had never
guessed at, in the arrangement of a home. She
was but half an hour in his company, and still
smiling, still full of words, she went away. He was
to see her again in a very short time; he was to
lunch at their house, and he stood for a moment
after the door had shut in the silence of the big
place, as though wondering how he should pass his
time. The hall in which he lingered was surely very
desolate; the bare boards he was sure he would
remember, however well they were covered; he
never could make those cold walls look warm. . . .
Anyhow, one didn't live in one's hall. He just
plodded upstairs slowly to what had been the draw-
ing-room of the house, and the big brass curtain
rods offended him; the rings were still upon them.
He would move them away, but still they offended
him. The lines were too regular, and there was
too little to appeal to him. He hesitated for a
moment as to whether he would go up farther and
look again at the upper rooms which they had discussed together, but the great well of the staircase
looked emptier than all the rest; the great mournful windows, filled with a grey northern sky, lit it,
but gave it no light. And he noticed, as he trod
the bare wood of the last flight, how dismally his

footsteps echoed. Then he called up the caretaker and gave her the key, surprised her with a considerable fee, and said he would communicate that day with the agents, and left.

When he got to lunch at his friends' house he told them that he would not take the Empty House after all, whereat they all buzzed with excitement, and asked him what he had found at the last moment. And he said, in a silly sort of way, that it was not haunted enough for him. But anyhow he did not take it : he went back to live in his rooms, and he lives there still.

The Landfall   ~   ~   ~   ~   ~

I T was in Oxford Street and upon the top of an
omnibus during one of those despairing winter
days, the light just gone, and an air rising which
was neither vigorous nor cold, but sodden like the
hearts of all around, that I fell wondering whether
there were some ultimate goal for men, and whether
these adventures of ours, which grow tamer and so
much tamer as the years proceed, are lost at last in
a blank nothingness, or whether there are revelations and discoveries to come. This debate in the
mind is very old; every man revolves it, none has
affirmed a solution, though all the wisest of men
have accepted a received answer from authority external to themselves. I was not on that murky
evening concerned with authority, but with the old
problem or rather mood of wonder upon the fate of
the soul.

As I so mused to the jolting of the bus I began
unconsciously to compare the keenness of early living
with the satiety or weariness of later years; and so
from one thing to another, I know not how, I
thought of horses first, and then of summer rivers,
and then of a harbour, and then of the open sea,
and then of the sea at night, till this vague train

The Landfall

took on the form of an exact picture, and my mind lived in an unforgotten day.

.   .   .   ,   .   .

In my little boat, with my companion asleep in the bows, I steered at the end of darkness eastward over a warm and easy sea.

It was August: the roll was lazy, and the stars were few and distant all around, because the sky, though clear, was softened by the pleasant air of summer at its close; moreover, an arch of the sky before me was paling and the sea-breeze smelt of dawn.

My little boat went easy, as the sea was easy. There was just enough of a following wind dead west to keep her steady and to keep the boom square in its place right out a-lee, nor did she shake or swing (as boats so often will before a following wind), but went on with a purpose gently, like a young woman just grown used to her husband and her home. So she sailed, and aft we left a little, bubbling wake, which in the darkness had glimmered with evanescent and magic fires, but now, as the morning broadened, could be seen to be white foam. The stars paled for an hour and then soon vanished; although the sun had not yet risen, it was day.

The line of the horizon before me was fresh and sharp, clear tops of swell showed hard against the faint blue of the lowest sky, and for some time we were thus alone together in the united and living immensity of the sea: my sleeping companion, my boat, and I. Then it was that I perceived a little northward and to the left of the rising glow a fixed appearance very far away beyond the edge of the world; it was grey and watery like a smoke, yet fixed in outline and unchanging; it did not waver but stood, and so standing confirmed its presence. It was land; and this dim but certain vision which now fixed my gaze was one of the mighty headlands of holy Ireland.

The noble hill lifted its mass upon the extreme limits of sight, almost dissolved by distance and yet clear; its summit was high and plain, and in the moment it was perceived the sea became a new thing. It was no longer void or absorbing, but became familiar water neighbourly to men; and was now that ocean, whose duty and meaning it is to stream around and guard the shores on which are founded cities and armies, families and enduring homes. The little boat sailed on, now in the mood for companions and for friends.

My companion stirred and woke; he raised himself upon his arm, and, looking forward to the left and right, at last said, "Land!" I told him the name of the headland. But I did not know that there lay beyond it a long and narrow bay, nor how, at the foot of this land-locked water, a group of small white houses stood, and behind it a very venerable tower.

The Landfall

It was not long before the sun came up out of a
sea more clear and into a sky more vivid than you
will see within the soundings of the Channel. It
poured upon all the hills an enlivening new light
quite different from the dawn, and this was especially noticeable upon the swell and the little ridges
of it, which danced and shone so that one thought
of music.

Meanwhile the land grew longer before us and
this one headland merged into the general line,
and inland heights could be seen; a little later
again it first became possible to distinguish the
divisions of the fields and the separate colours of
rocks and of grassland and of trees. A little while
later again the white thread showed all along that
coast where the water broke at the meeting of the
rocks and the sea; the tide was at the flood.

We had, perhaps, three miles between us and the
land (where every detail now stood out quite sharp
and clear) when the wind freshened suddenly and,
after the boat had heeled as suddenly and run for a
moment with the scuppers under, she recovered and
bounded forward. It was like obedience to a call, or
like the look that comes suddenly into men's eyes
when they hear unexpectedly a familiar name. She
lifted at it and she took the sea, for the sea began to
rise.

Then there began that dance of vigour which is
almost a combat, when men sail with skill and under
some stress of attention and of danger. I would not

take in an inch because of the pleasure of it, but she
was over-canvased all the same, and I put her ever
so little round for fear of a gybe, but the pleasure of
it was greater than the fear, and the cordage sang,
and it gave me delight to glance over my shoulder
at that following rush which chases a small boat
always when she presses before a breeze and might
poop her if her rider did not know his game. That
which had been a long, long sail through the night
with an almost silent wake and the bursting of but
few bubbles, and next a steady approach before the
strong and easy wind, had now become something
inspired and exultant, a course which resembled a
charge ; and the more the sea rose the larger everything became—the boat's career, the land upon
which she was determined, and our own minds,
while all about us as we urged and raced for shore
were the loud noises of the sea.

We ran straight for a point where could be seen
the gate to the inland bay ; we rounded it, and our
entry completed all, for when once we had rounded
the point all fell together ; the wind, the heaving
of the water, the sounds and the straining of the
sheets. In a moment, and less than a moment, we
had cut out from us the vision of the sea, a barrier
of cliff and hill stood between us and the large
horizon. The very lonely slopes of these western
mountains rose solemn and enormous all around, and
the bay on which we floated, with only just that way
which remained after our sharp turning, was quite

The Landfall

lucid and clear, like the seas by southern beaches where one can look down and see a world underneath our own. The boom swung inboard, the canvas hung in folds, and my companion forward cut loose the little anchor from its tie, the chain went rattling down, and so silent was that sacred place that one could hear an echo from the cliffs close by returning the clanking of the links; the chain ran out and slowly tautened as she fell back and rode to it. Then we let go the halyards, and when the slight creaking of the blocks had ceased there was no more noise. Everything was still.

.   .   .   .   .   .

There was the vision that returned to me.

I was in the midst of it, I was almost present, I had forgotten the streets of the treacherous and evil town, when suddenly, I know not what, a cry, or some sharp movement near me, brought me back from such a place and day, from such an experience, such a parallel and such a security.

With that return to the common business of living the thought on which my mind had begun its travel also returned, but in spite of the mood I had so recently enjoyed my doubts were not resolved.

The Little Old Man ⌁ ⌁ ⌁ ⌁

IT was in the year 1888 ("O noctes coenasque deum!"—a tag) that, upon one of the southern hills of England, I came quite unexpectedly across a little old man who sat upon a bench that was there and looked out to sea.

Now you will ask me why a bench was there, since benches are not commonly found upon the high slopes of our southern hills, of which the poet has well said, the writer has well written, and the singer has well sung :—

> The Southern Hills and the South Sea
> They blow such gladness into me
> That when I get to Burton Sands
> And smell the smell of the home lands,
> My heart is all renewed, and fills
> With the Southern Sea and the South Hills.

True, benches are not common there. I know of but one, all the way from the meeting place of England, which is upon Salisbury Plain, to that detestable suburb of Eastbourne by Beachy Head. Nay, even that one of which I speak has disappeared. For an honest man being weary of labour and yet desiring firewood one day took it away, and the stumps only now remain at the edge of a wood, a little to the south of No Man's Land.

The Little Old Man

Well, at any rate, upon this bench there sat in the year 1888 a little old man, and he was looking out to sea; for from this place the English Channel spreads out in a vast band 600ft. below one, and the shore perhaps five miles away; it looks broader than any sea in the world, broader than the Mediterranean from the hills of Alba Longa, and broader than the Irish Sea from the summit of the Welsh Mountains: though why this is so I cannot tell. The little old man treated my coming as though it was an expected thing, and before I had spoken to him long assured me that this view gave him complete content.

" I could sit here," he said, " and look at the Channel and consider the nature of this land for ever and for ever." Now though words like this meant nothing in so early a year as the year 1888, yet I was willing to pursue them because there was, in the eyes of the little old man, a look of such wisdom, kindness, and cunning as seemed to me a marriage between those things native to the earth and those things which are divine. I mean, that he seemed to me to have all that the good animals have, which wander about in the brushwood and are happy all their lives, and also all that we have, of whom it has been well said that of every thing which runs or creeps upon earth, man is the fullest of sorrow. For this little old man seemed to have (at least such was my fantastic thought in that early year) a complete acquiescence in the soil and the air that had bred him, and

23

yet something common to mankind and a full fore-knowledge of death.

His face was of the sort which you will only see in England, being quizzical and vivacious, a little pinched together, and the hair on his head was a close mass of grey curls. His eyes were as bright as are harbour lights when they are first lit towards the closing of our winter evenings : they shone upon the daylight. His mouth was firm, but even in repose it permanently, though very slightly, smiled.

I asked him why he took such pleasure in the view. He said it was because everything he saw was a part of his own country, and that just as some holy men said that to be united with God, our Author, was the end and summit of man's effort, so to him who was not very holy, to mix, and have communion, with his own sky and earth was the one banquet that he knew : he also told me (which cheered me greatly) that alone of all the appetites this large affection for one's own land does not grow less with age, but rather increases and occupies the soul. He then made me a discourse as old men will, which ran somewhat thus :—

"Each thing differs from all others, and the more you know, the more you desire or worship one thing, the more does that stand separate : and this is a mystery, for in spite of so much individuality all things are one. . . . How greatly out of all the world stands out this object of my adoration and of my content! you will not find the like of it in all the world! It is England, and in the love of it I forget all enmities and all despairs."

He then bade me look at a number of little things around, and see how particular they were : the way in which the homes of Englishmen hid themselves, and how, although a great town lay somewhat to our right not half a march away, there was all about us silence, self-possession, and repose. He bade me also note the wind-blown thorns, and the yew-trees, bent over from centuries of the south-west wind, and the short, sweet grass of the Downs, untilled and unenclosed, and the long waves of woods which rich men had stolen and owned, and which yet in a way were property for us all.

"There is more than one," said I in anger, "who so little understands his land that he will fence the woods about and prevent the people from coming and going : making a show of them, like some dirty town-bred fellow who thinks that the Downs and the woods are his villa-garden, bought with gold."

The little old man wagged his crooked forefinger in front of his face and looked exceedingly knowing with his bright eyes, and said : "Time will tame all that! Not they can digest the county, but the county them. Their palings shall be burnt upon cottage hearths, and their sons shall go back to be lackeys as their fathers were. But this landscape shall always remain."

Then he bade me note the tides and the many harbours ; and how there was an inner and an outer tide, and the great change between neaps and springs, and how there were no great rivers, but every harbour stood right upon the sea, and how for the knowledge of each of these harbours even the life of a man was too short. There was no other country, he said, which was thus held and embraced by the mastery of the Atlantic tide. For the patient Dutch have their towns inland upon broad rivers and ships sail up to quays between houses or between green fields; and the Spaniards and the French (he said) are, for half their nature and tradition, taught by a tideless sea, but we all around have the tide everywhere, and with the tide there comes to character salt and variety, adventure, peril, and change.

" But this," I said, " is truer of the Irish."

He answered : " Yes, but I am talking of my own soil."

Then when he had been silent for a little while he began talking of the roads, which fitted into the folds of the hills, and of the low long window panes of men's homes, of the deep thatch which covered them, and of that savour of fullness and inheritance which lay fruitfully over all the land. It gave him the pleasure to talk of these things which it gives men who know particular wines to talk of those wines, or men who have enjoyed some great risk together to talk together of their dangers overcome.

It gave him the same pleasure to talk of England and of his corner of England that it gives some venerable people sometimes to talk of those whom

The Little Old Man

they have loved in youth, or that it gives the true
poets to mouth the lines of their immortal peers. It
was a satisfaction to hear him say the things he said,
because one knew that as he said them his soul was
filled.

He spoke also of horses and of the birds native to
our Downs, but not of pheasants, which he hated and
would not speak to me about at all. He spoke of
dogs, and told me how the dogs of one countryside
were the fruits of it, just as its climate and its con-
tours were; notably the spaniel, which was designed
or bred by the mighty power of Amberley Wildbrook,
which breeds all watery things. He showed me how
the plover went with the waste flats of Arun and of
Adur and of Ouse, and he showed me why the sheep
were white and why they bunched together in a
herd. "Because," he said, "the chalk pits and the
clouds behind the Down are wide patches of white;
so must the sheep be also." For a little he would
have told me that the very names of places, nay, the
religion itself, were grown right out of the sacred
earth which was our Mother.

.   .   .   .   .   .

These truths and many more I should have learned
from him, these extravagences and some few others
I should have whimsically heard, had I not (since I
was young) attempted argument and said to him:
" But all these things change, and what we love so
much is. after all, only what we have known in our

short time, and it is our souls within that lend divin-
ity to any place, for, save within the soul, all is
subject to time."

He shook his head determinedly and like one who
knows. He did assure me that in a subtle master-
ing manner the land that bore us made us ourselves,
and was the major and the dominant power which
moulded, as with firm hands, the clay of our being
and which designed and gave us, and continued in us,
all the form in which we are.

"You cannot tell this," I said, "and neither can
I ; it is all guesswork to the brevity of man."

"You are wrong," he answered quietly. "I have
watched these things for quite 3000 years." And
before I had time to gasp at that word he had
disappeared.

The Long March ∽ ∽ ∽ ∽

THE French Service, by some superstition of
theirs which is probably connected with clear
thinking and with decision, have perpetually in
mind two things where Infantry is (or are) concerned; these two things are, marching power and
carrying weight.

It is their thesis, or rather it is their general
opinion, that of all things in which civilised armies
may differ the power of trained endurance is the
most variable, and that the elements in which this
endurance is most usefully manifested are the elements of bearing a weight for long and of marching
for long and far between a sleep and a sleep.

There is no Service in the world but would agree
that rapidity of movement (other things being equal)
is to the advantage of an army. Not even the Blue
Water School (for which school armies are distant
and vague things) would deny that. It is even true
that most men (though by no means all) who have
to do with thinking out military problems would
admit that, other things again being equal, the
power of carrying weight was an advantage to an
army. But the French Service differs from its rivals
in this, that it regards these two factors in a sort of

fundamental way, testing the whole Army by them and keeping them perpetually present before the whole of that Army, so that the stupidest driver in front of the guns is worrying in a muddled way as to whether the Line have not too much to do, and the cleverest young captain on the staff is wondering whether the strain put upon a particular regiment has not been too great that day. The exercise is continual, and is made as much a part of the men's mode of thought as cricket is made a part of the mode of thought of a boy at school, or as the daily paper is made a part of the mode of thought of a man who comes in daily from the suburbs to gamble in the City of London. And the French Service shows its permeation in the matter of these two ideas by this very characteristic test, that not only are the supporters of either element in the power of Infantry numerous and enthusiastic, but also that those (and I believe for a moment Negrier) who think these theories have been overdone recognise at the back of their minds the general importance of them; while the great neutral mass that sometimes discuss, but hardly ever think originally, take them as it were for granted in all their discussions.

It would be possible to continue for some time the exposition of this most interesting thing; it would be possible to show how this point of view was con- nected with the conservatism of the French mind. It would be possible and fascinating perhaps to show the relation of such theories with the mentality

The Long March

which is convinced upon the retention of private property and upon the subdivision of it, upon the all-importance of agriculture to a State, upon the possession at no matter what sacrifice of a vast amount of vaulted, tangible, material gold. But my business in these lines is not to argue whether the French are right or wrong in this military aspect of their philosophy, nor to show them wise or unwise in regarding even the railways of a modern State as being only supplementary to marching power, and even the vast and mobile modern methods of road carriage as being only supplementary to the knapsack, which can go across ploughed fields or climb a tree. My business is not to discuss the philosophy of the thing, though I am grievously tempted to do so, but to speak of one particular thing I saw.

I saw the beginning, the middle, and the end of it. Had I myself been in the Line such things might have been so familiar to me that they would not in the long run have stood out in my imagination, and I might not have been as fascinated as I now am by the recollections of that strange experience.

The Infantry that was the support of our pieces (for we were Divisionary Artillery) was quartered near to us in a little village of what is called "the Champagne Pouilleuse," that is, "the lousy," or "the dusty" Champagne, to distinguish it from the chalky range of the mountain of Rheims, those hot slopes whereon is grown the grape producing the most northern and the most exhilarating of wines.

31

On Everything

In this little village were we side by side, and very far off along the horizon we had seen the night before, to the north, guns and linesmen together, the goal of our journey, which was that roll in the ground upon the summit of which the very tall spire of a famous shrine led the eye on toward the larger mass of the Cathedral. The Road was straight both upon the map and in our weary minds. It crossed the fields on which had been decided the fate of Christendom in the defeat of Attila and again in the cannonade of Valmy. Little we cared for these things. What we cared about, or rather what the fellows on foot cared about, was a distance of nearly thirty miles with fifty pound and more upon one's back.

I lay in the straw of the stable near my horses, whose names were Pacte and Basilique—Basilique was the elder one and was ridden, and Pacte was the led horse—when I heard the sound of a bugle. I was already awake, I cannot tell why, I had no duties; I strolled out from the stable into the square and watched the Line assembling. They were of all sorts and sizes in the dark morning, for the French are profoundly indifferent to making a squad look neat. Some shuffled, others ran, others affected to saunter to where the sergeant, with the roll in his hand and a lantern held above it, stood ready to call out the names. As they gathered to fall in I heard their comments, which were familiar enough, for they did not differ from the comments we also made when any effort was required of us. They cursed all order and discipline. Some boasted that the thing was not tolerable, and that they were the men to make the system impossible. Others cunningly hinted that they would deceive the doctor and fall out, and in general it would have been conceded by any man listening to them that this march could never be accomplished.

With the usual oaths, dreadful to an intellectual ear, but to us a sort of atmosphere, they fell in, and all over the village square were other companies falling in and other sergeants holding other rolls. Then the names were called, with no trappings, in a rather low voice, and rapidly.

One man was missing, and the sergeant looked round, saw me leaning against my stable door, and told me to go for the guard; but when I had got four men from the guard the missing man had come up. He was a very little man, in a hurry; he was not punished, he was warned. Hardly had I returned and hardly had the four men of the guard (who that day of the march were Cavalry) gone back straggling when the various companies shuffled into place, formed fours, and began the marching column. No drums rolled, no bugle inspirited them. The little village was now more clearly seen under a growing light, and there were bands of colour above the distant ridge of the Argonne. It was not quite four in the morning, and there was a mist from the meadows beside the road.

On Everything

They went out silently. There was a sort of step kept, but it was very loose. They sang no songs, they were a most unfortunate crowd.

$$\cdot \qquad \cdot \qquad \cdot \qquad \cdot \qquad \cdot \qquad \cdot$$

We had been for two hours upon our horses, we who had started long after sunrise after our horses had been groomed and fed and watered, and treated like Christian men—for it was a saying of ours that the Republic was kinder to a horse than to a man, because a horse cost money. We had gone, I said, two hours also along the road, trotting and walking alternately, with the interminable clatter-clank-clank of the limber and the pieces behind us, and with the occasional oath of the sergeant or the corporal when a trace went loose or when a bit of bad riding on the part of some leader checked the column of guns; we had so pounded along into the heat of the day; the sun was beginning to offend us—we were more in a sweat than our horses—when we heard a long way off upon the road before us the faint noise of a song, and soon we saw from one of those recurring summits of the arrow-like French road, the jolly fellows of the Line. They were not more than a thousand yards before us; they made a little dust as they went, and as they went their rifles swinging on the shoulder gave them a false appearance of unity—for unity they were not caring at all. Somewhat before we reached them we saw their cohesion break, they became a doubled mob

34

upon either side of the road, and we knew that they
were making the regulation halt of five minutes,
which is ordered at the end of every hour; but
probably their commanding officer had somewhat
advanced or retarded this in order to make a coincidence with the going by of the guns.

We saw them as we approached lying in all atti-
tudes upon either side of the road, some few munching
bread from the haversack, and some few drinking
from their gourds. As we came up they were compelled to rise to salute another arm upon its passage,
and their faces, all their double hedge of faces, were
full of insolence and of merriment, for they had
recently sung and eaten, and the march had done
them good—they had covered about eighteen miles.

So we went by, and when we had left them some
few hundred yards we again heard faintly behind us
the beginning of a new song, the tune of which was
known among us as "The Washerwoman." It is a
good marching song. But shortly after this we heard
no more, for first the noise of the horse hoofs extinguished the singing, and later distance swallowed it
up altogether.

.   .   .   .   .   .

We had come into quarters early in the afternoon,
we had groomed our horses and fed them, and
watered them at the chalkiest stream, we had
brought them back to their stables, and the stable
guard was set; those who were not on duty went off

about the village, and several, of whom I was one,
gathered in the house of a man whose relative in the
regiment had led us thither.

He received us well, for he was a farmer in a large
way; he gave us wine, bread, and eggs, and a little
bacon. He said he hoped that no more troops would
come into the little village that day. We told him
that the Line would come, so far as we knew, but he
answered that he had heard from his brother, who
was mayor of the adjoining commune, that the Line
were to be quartered in that neighbouring parish,
that they would march through the village in which
we were, and sleep in the houses about a mile ahead
of us upon the road to Rheims.

While he was speaking thus we heard again, but
much louder than before (for it came upon us round
the corner of the village street), the noise of a marching song. They were singing at the top of their
voices—they were in a sort of fury of singing.

They passed along making more dust than ever
before, and anyone who had not known them would
have said they were out of hand. Several were
limping as they went, one or two, recognising the
gunners and the drivers, waved their hands. The
rest still sang. No one had fallen out. Their arms
they carried anyhow, and more than one man was
carrying two rifles (probably for money), and more
than one man was carrying none, and some had their
rifles slung across their backs, and some tucked under
their arms. So they went forward, and again we

heard their singing dwindle, but this time it continued much longer than before, and I think we heard it up to the halt, when their task was accomplished and the march was done.

They are an incredible people !

On Saturnalia ∾ ∾ ∾ ∾ ∾

ONE of the bothers of writing is that words carry
about upon their backs nowadays a great pack
of past meanings and derivations, and that—particularly to-day—no word is standing still as it were
and meaning something once and for all which a
plain man can say without being laughed at for
ignorance or for affectation. For instance, Saturnalia. To one man it means a certain bundle of
ritual many centuries dead, common to a particular
district of Italy and practised in midwinter. To
another man it means a lot of poor people having an
exaggerated beanfeast and thereby annoying the
rich people. But it does not mean either of these
things to the plain man. It means to the plain man
occasion and specific occasion for turning things
upside down and getting breathing space for a
while from the crushing order of this world. That
is what "Saturnalia" means to the ordinary user of
the word, and note, he has no other word by which
to express the idea—so thoroughly has the thing
died out since modern English was formed. I suppose the nearest word for it in English—when such
feasts were still known in England—was the vague

On Saturnalia

word "Misrule." Anyhow, it is Saturnalia now, and Saturnalia it shall be here.

If a man were to come back from the past and watch the modern world into which he had tumbled he would note any number of things that would, I am certain, intoxicate him with wonder and delight. Just as one is intoxicated with wonder and delight on landing in youth upon the quays of a foreign port for the first time—that is, if the foreign port is well governed, for there is no wonder or delight either in barbarism or in decay. Such a man would be perpetually running to telephones, those curious toys, and marvelling at cinematographs and rejoicing in express trains and clear print and big guns and phonographs; he couldn't help it. Motor-cars moving by themselves would fill him with magic—but he would bitterly mislike certain absences, and he would complain that half a dozen things were very wrong with the world. So many men free and yet owning nothing—so much the greater part of men free and yet owning nothing—would seem to him a monstrous and perilous thing. The exact and mechanical accuracy that clocks and railways have made would offend him; he would see it as a disease wearing out men's nerves. The modern arguments all in a circle round and round the old insoluble problems would bore him dreadfully, and still more perhaps the fresh discoveries every week of principles and plain truths as old as the Mediterranean—but nothing surely would astonish him or grieve him or frighten him more than the absence of topsy-turvydom without some recurrent breath of which the soul of man perishes.

And why? There is a question you may ask some time before it will be answered. One thing is sure, though the sureness of it reposes on some base we cannot see : in the proportion that men are secure of their philosophy and social scheme, in that proportion they must in some fixed manner turn it upside down from time to time for their delight and show it on a stage or enact it in a religious ritual with all its rules reversed and the whole thing wrong way about. They have always done this in healthy States, and if ever our State gets healthy they will begin to do it again. It is a human craving, an intense craving—but why, it would be a business to say.

It must not be imagined that the craving or the expression of it has passed from us to-day. They have no more passed from us than the desire for property or for the tilling of the land. But their corporate character is broken up, they appear sporadically in individuals only, and are therefore often evil. They appear in the irony which is an increasing feature of our letters, in mad freaks and outbreaks for which men strained beyond bearing are punished, and they appear in fantastic prophecies of a changed world.

One sees that craving for a burst of misrule in quite unexpected enthusiasms for things remote

from our lives, in great senseless mobs furious about
minor things—the minor actions of a campaign or
the minor details of law-making—in the public
clamour about the misfortunes of some foreign
prisoner or the politics of some alien State. One
sees it in the men who suddenly start rules of life
based on some careful negation of what all around
them do, in the leaders and teachers who first note
exactly what nearly all their fellow-beings eat or
drink or wear, and then most loudly proclaim salva-
tion to lie in *not* eating, drinking, or wearing these
obviously necessary things. The neighbours stare!
And no wonder—for private Saturnalia are danger-
ously near to vice in the sane, in the weak to
insanity.

But true Saturnalia, public Saturnalia, were
healthy because they were corporate. Custom and
religion had dug a sort of channel into which all
that emotion could commonly run, and in midwinter,
when it had long been very dark, the mischiefs, the
comic spirits came out of the woods and for some
days possessed the souls of men, and these, by that
possession, were purged and freed. So it was for
hundreds upon hundreds of years—until quite the
modern time. Why have we lost it, and how long
must we wait for it to return?

When the relations of slave and master seemed
as obvious and necessary as seem to us (let us say)
the reading of a daily paper or the taking of a
train, yet the obvious and necessary routine was

On Everything

broken in midwinter, the slave was the master for a moment and the master a slave.

When the ritual of the Church was as much a commonplace as the ritual of social life is to us to-day, there was a season (it was this season between Christmas and the Epiphany) when the dead weight of order was lifted and a boy was dressed as a bishop or a donkey was put to chaunt the office, and the people sang :—

> Plebs autem respondet :
> Hé sire Ane, ho ! Chantez !
> Vous aurez du foin assez
> Et de l'avoine à manger !

When the awful authority of civil and hereditary powers was unquestioned they yet set up in English halls Lords of Misrule who governed that season. The Inns of Court, I believe, delighted in them, and certainly till quite late in the seventeenth century the peasantry of the villages.

It has gone. It will return. During its absence (and may that absence not be much prolonged) perhaps one can see its nature the more clearly because one sees it from the outside and as a distant though a desired thing. Perhaps we, living in a very unreasonable age, when realities are forgotten and imaginaries preferred, when we solemnly reiterate impossibilities, affirm our faith in scientific guesswork and our doubts upon the plain rules of arithmetic, can understand why our much more reasonable fathers thirsted for and obtained these feasts of un-

On Saturnalia

reason. It seems to have been a little like the natural craving for temporary oblivion (sleep—a chaos) once in every day; a sort of bath in that muddle or nothingness out of which the world was made. Equality, which lies at the base of society, was brought to surface by a paradox and shown at large. Intensity of conviction and of organisation took refuge in the relief of a momentary—and not meant—denial of that conviction and organisation, and the whole of society collectively expanded its soul by one collective foolery at high pressure, as does the healthy individual by one good farce or peal of laughter when occasion serves.

How the Saturnalia will return (as return they will) no one can say. The seeds of reaction from the tangle of the modern world lie all around in the customs and the demands of the populace : but seeds are never known or perceived till they have sprouted. Sometimes one catches the echo of the return in a chance jest; especially if it be a cabman's. Sometimes in a solemn hoax largely indulged in by many poor men against one richer than themselves. Sometimes in the voluntary humour and cynical goodness of heart of a powerful or wealthy man exposing the illusions of his kind.

Anyhow, one way or another, sooner or later, the Saturnalia will return ; may it be sooner rather than later, and at the latest not later than 1938, when so many of us will be so very old.

On Everything

For my part I shall look for the first signs in the provinces of rich and riotous blood as on the Border (and especially just north of it) or in Flanders, or, better still, in Burgundy from Nuits and Beaune northward and eastward. I have especially great hopes of the town of Dijon.

A Little Conversation in Herefordshire ∽

THERE is a country house (as the English phrase goes) in the County of Hereford, at a little distance from the River Wye ; the people who live in this house are very rich. They are not rich precariously, nor with doubts here and there, nor for the time, but in a solid manner ; that is, they believe their riches to be eternal. Their income springs from very many places, of which they have not an idea ; it is spent in a straightforward manner, which they fully comprehend. It is spent in relieving the incompetence—the economic incompetence—of all those about them ; in causing wine to come into England from Ay, Vosne, Barsac, and (though they do not know it) from the rougher soil of Algiers. It also causes (does the way in which they exercise what only pedants call their Potential Demand) tea to be grown in Ceylon for their servants and in China for themselves, horses to be bred in Ireland, and wheat to be sown and most laboriously garnered in Western Canada, Ohio, India, South Russia, the Argentine, and other places. Also, were you to seek out every economic cause and effect, you would find missionaries living where no man can live, save by artifice, and living upon artificial supply in a strange climate

45

by the strength of this Potential Demand rooted in the meadows of the Welsh March.

Then, also, if you were to follow the places whence their wealth is derived, it would interest you very much. You would see one man earning so much in the docks and handing on a Saturday evening so much of his wages into their fund. You would see another clipping off cloth in Manchester and offering it to them, and another plucking cotton in Egypt and exchanging it, at their order, against something which they, not he, needed. Altogether you would see the whole world paying tithe, and a stream flowing into Hereford as into a reservoir, and a stream flowing out again by many channels.

These good people were at dinner ; upon the 5th of October, to be accurate. Parliament had not yet met, but football had begun, and there was shooting, also a little riding upon horses, though this is not to-day a popular amusement, and few will practise it. As for the women, one wrote and the other read— which was a fair division of labour ; but the woman who wrote was not read by the woman who read, for the woman who wrote (and she was the daughter) preferred to write upon problems. But her mother, who did the reading, preferred what is called fiction, and Mr. Meredith was a favourite author of hers ; but, indeed, she would read all fiction so only that it was in her native tongue.

Now the men of the family were very different from this, and the things they liked were hunting of

A Little Conversation in Herefordshire

a particular kind (which I shall not here describe),
shooting of a similar kind, their country, and politics,
which last interest it would have been abominable to
deny them, for the two men, both father and son,
were actively engaged in the making of laws, each in
a different place ; the laws they made (it is true in
the company of, and with the advice of, others) are
to be found in what is called the Statute Book, which
neither you nor I have ever seen.

All these four, the father, the son, the mother, and
the daughter, in different ways intelligent, but all
four very kind and good, were at dinner upon this
day of which I speak, the 5th of October, but they
were not alone. They had to meet them several
people who were staying in the house. The one was
a satirist who had been born in Lithuania. He was
poor and proud and had learnt the English tongue,
and he wrote books upon the pride of race and upon
battling with the sea. He was an envious sort of
man, but as he never had nor ever would have any
home or lineage, England was much the same to him
as any other place. He hated all our nations with
an equal hatred.

Another guest was a little man called Copp. He
was a lord ; his title was not Copp. Only his name
was Copp, and even this name he hid, for old father
Copp, who had married a Miss Billings in the eighteenth century, had had a son John Billings, since the
Billings were richer than the Copps. And John
Billings had married Mary Steyning, who was the

Squire's daughter, and they had had a son John
Steyning, since John was by this time the hereditary
name. Now John Steyning was in the Parliament
that worked for the Regent, and a short one it was,
and he became plain Lord Steyning, and then he
and his son and his grandson married in all sorts
of ways, and the title now was Bramber, but the
family name was Steyning, and the real name was
Copp. So much for Copp. He was as lively as a
grig, he had travelled everywhere, and he knew
about ten languages. He was peculiarly brave,
and as a boy he had stoutly refused to go to the
University.

Then also there was the Doctor, who was absurdly
nervous and could ill afford to dine out, and there
was a young man who was in Parliament with the
son of the family; this young man had been to Oxford
with him also, not at Cambridge; he was a lawyer,
and he was making three thousand pounds a year,
but he said he was making six when he talked to his
wife and mother, and most serious men believed that
he was making ten. The women of these were also
present with them, saving always that Copp, who
was called Steyning, and whose title was Bramber,
was not married.

These then, sitting round the table, came to talk
of something after all not remote from the interest
of their lives. They talked of Socialists, and it all
began by Copp (who called himself Steyning, while
his title was Bramber) saying that his uncle Gwil-

liam had just missed being a Socialist because he
was too stupid.

The Head of the Family, who had most imperfectly caught the pronouncement of Copp as to his
relative, said, " Yes, Bramber; got to be pretty
stupid to be that! " By which the Head of the
House meant that one had to be pretty stupid to be
a Socialist, whereas what Copp had said was that
his uncle had been too stupid to be a Socialist. But
it was all one.

The Son of the House said that there were lots
of Socialists going about, and the young lawyer
friend said there were a lot of people who said
they were Socialists but who were not Socialists.

The Daughter of the House said that it was very
interesting the way in which Socialism went up and
down. She said: " Look at the Fabians! " The
Mother of the House looked all round, smiling
genially, for she thought that her daughter was
speaking of the name of a book.

The Doctor said: " It's all a pose, those sort of
people." But which sort he did not say, so the
Daughter of the House said sharply : " Which sort
of people? " For she loved to cross-examine struggling professional men, and the Doctor got quite
red, and said; " Oh, all that sort of people ! "

The young lawyer, who was quick to see a
difficulty, helped him out by saying, " He means
people like Bensington! '

The Doctor, who had never heard of Bensington,

nodded eagerly, and the **Head** of the House frowning a healthy frown, said, "What, not John Bensington, old William Bensington's son?"

"Yes," said the young lawyer. "That's the kind of man he means," and the Doctor nodded again.

His enemy was dropping farther and farther behind him with every stride, but she made a brilliant rally. "Do you mean John Bensington?" she said. The Doctor, in some alarm, and with his mouth full, nodded vigorously for the third time. The Head of the House, still frowning, broke into all this with a solid roar: "I don't believe a word of it." He sat leaning back again, not relaxing his frown and trying to connect the son of his old friend with a gang of treasonable robbers. He remembered Jock's marriage—for it was a bad one—and a silly book of verses he had written, and how keen he had been against his father's selling the bit of land along the coast, because it was bound to go up. He could fit Jock in with many unpleasant things, but he couldn't fit him in with the very definite picture that rose in his mind whenever he heard the word "Socialist." There was something adventurous and violent and lean about the word—something like a wolf. There was nothing of all that in Jock. So much thought matured at last into living words, and the Head of the House said, "Why, he's on the County Council."

The Daughter of the House turned to the lawyer

A Little Conversation in Herefordshire

and said, "How would you define a Socialist, Mr. Layton?"

Mr. Layton defined a Socialist, and his silent wife, who was sitting opposite, looked at him happily on account of the power of his mind. The Lithuanian, who had said nothing all this while, but had been glancing with eyes as bright as a bird's, now at one speaker, now at another, nerved himself to intervene. Then there passed over his little soul the vivid pictures of things he had seen and known: the dens in Riga, the pain, the flight upon a Danish ship, the assumption first of German, then of English nationality, the easy gullibility of the large-hearted wealthy people of this land. He remembered his own confidence, his own unwavering talent, and his contempt of, and hatred for, other men. He could have trusted himself to speak, for he was in full command of his little soul, and there was not a trace of anything in his accent definitely foreign. But the virtue and the folly of these happy luxurious people about him pleased him too much and pleased him wickedly.

He went on tasting them in silence, until the Daughter of the House, who felt awe for him alone of all those present—much more awe than she did for her strong and good father—said to him, almost with reverence, that he should take to writing now of the meadows of England, since he had so wonderfully described her battles at sea. And the Lithuanian was ready to turn the talk upon letters,

his bright eyes darting all the while.   The old man,
the Head of the House, sighed and muttered:
"Jock was no Socialist."   That was the one thing
that he retained; . . . and meanwhile wealth continued to pour in from all corners of the world into
his house, and to pour out again over the four seas,
doing his will, and no one in the world, not even
the chief victims of that wealth, hated it as the
little Lithuanian did, and no one in the world—not
even of them who had seen most of that wealth—
hungered bestially for it as did he.

On the Rights of Property ∾　∾　∾

THERE is in the dark heart of Soho, not far from a large stable where Zebras, Elephants, and trained Ponies await their turn for the footlights and the inebriation of public applause, a little tavern, divided, as are even the meanest of our taverns, into numerous compartments, each corresponding to some grade in the hierarchy of our ancient and orderly society.

For many years the highest of these had been called "the Private Bar," and was distinguished from its next fellow by this, that the cushions upon its little bench were covered with sodden velvet, not with oilcloth. Here, also, the drink provided by the politician who owned this and many other public-houses was served in glasses of uncertain size and not by imperial measure. This, I say, had been the chief or summit of the place for many years; from the year of the great Exhibition, in fact until that great change in London life which took place towards the end of the eighties and brought us, among other things, a new art and a new conception of world-wide power. In those years, as the mind of London changed so did this little public-house (which was called "the Lord

On Everything

Benthorpe "), and it added yet another step to its hierarchy of pens. This new place was called "the Saloon Bar." It was larger and better padded, and there was a tiny table in it. Then the years went on and wars were fought and the modern grip of man over natural forces marvellously extended, and the wealth of a world's Metropolis greatly swelled, and "The Lord Benthorpe" found room for yet another and final reserve wherein it might receive the very highest of its clients. This was built upon what had been the backyard, it had several tables, and it was called "the Lounge."

So far so good. Here late one evening when the music-halls had just discharged their thousands, and when the Elephants, the Zebras, and the Ponies near by were retiring to rest, sat two men, both authors ; the one was an author who had written for now many years upon social subjects, and notably upon the statistics of our industrial conditions. He had come nearer than any other to the determination of the Incidence of Economic Rent upon Retail Exchange and had been the first to show (in an essay, now famous) that the Ricardian Theory of Surplus did not apply in the anarchic competition of Retail Dealing, at least in our main thoroughfares.

His companion wielded the pen in another manner. It was his to analyse into its last threads of substance the human mind. Rare books proceeded from him at irregular and lengthy intervals packed with a close observation of the ultimate

On the Rights of Property

motives of men and an exact portrayal of their
labyrinth of deed; nor could he achieve his ideal in
this province of letters save by the use of words so
unusual and, above all, arranged in an order so peculiar to himself, as to bring upon his few readers
often perplexity and always awe.

Neither of these two men was wealthy. Such
incomes as they gained had not even that quality
of regular flow which, more than mere volume, impresses the years with security. Each was driven
to continual expedients, and each had lost such
careful habits as only a regular supply can per-
petuate. The consequence of this impediment was
apparent in the clothing of both men and in the
grooming of each; for the Economist, who was the
elder, wore a frock-coat unsuited to the occasion,
marked in many places with lighter patches against
its original black, and he had upon his head a top
hat of no great age and yet too familiar and rough,
and dusty at the brim. The Psychologist, upon the
other hand, sprawled in a suit of wool, grey and in
places green, which was most slipshod and looked
as though at times he slept in it, which indeed at
times he did. Unlike his elder companion he wore
no stiff collar round his throat, a negligence which
saved him from the reproach of frayed linen worn
through too many days; his shirt was a grey woollen
shirt with a grey woollen collar of such a sort as
scientific men assure us invigorates the natural func-
tions and prolongs the life of man.

On Everything

These two fell at once to a discussion upon that matter which absorbs the best of modern minds. I mean the organisation of Production in the modern world. It was their favourite theme. Their drink was Port, which, carelessly enough, they continued to order in small glasses instead of beginning boldly with the bottle. The Port was bad, or rather it was not Port, yet had they bought one bottle of it they would have saved the earnings of many days.

It was their favourite theme. . . . Each was possessed of an intellectual scorn for the mere ritual of an older time; neither descended to an affirmation nor even condescended to a denial of private property. Both clearly saw that no organised scheme of production could exist under modern conditions unless its organisation were to be controlled by the community. Yet the two friends differed in one most material point, which was the possibility, men being what they were, of settling thus the control of *machinery*. Upon land they were agreed. The land must necessarily be made a national thing, and the conception of ownership in it, however limited, was, as a man whom they both revered had put it, "unthinkable." Indeed, they recognised that the first steps towards so obvious a reform were now actually taken, and they confidently expected the final processes in it to be the work of quite the next few years; but whereas the Economist, with his profound knowledge of external detail, could see no obstacle to the collective control of capital as well, the Psychologist, ever dwelling upon the inner springs of action, saw no hope, no, not even for so evident and necessary a scheme, save in some ideal despotism of which he despaired. In vain did the Economist point out that our great railways, our mines, the main part of our shipping, and even half our textile industry had now no personal element in their direction save that of the salaried management; the Psychologist met him at every move with the effect produced upon man by the mere illusion of a personal element in all these things. The Economist, not a little inspired as the evening deepened, remembered and even invented names, figures, cases that showed the growing unity of the industrial world ; the Psychologist equally inspired, and with an equal increase of fervour, drew picture after picture, each more vivid and convincing than the last, of man caught in the tangle of imaginary motive and unobedient to any industrial control, unless that control could by some miracle be given the quality of universal tyranny.

Music was added to their debate, and subtly changed, as it must always change, the colour of thought. In the street without a man with a fine baritone voice, which evidently he had failed through vice or carelessness to exploit with success, sang songs of love and war, and at his side there accompanied him a little organ upon wheels which a weary woman played. The rich notes of his voice filled " The Lord Benthorpe " through the opened windows

of that hot night, and drowned or modified the differences of cabmen and others in the Public Bar ; as he
sang the two disputants rose almost to the lyric in
their enthusiasm, the one for the new world that was
so soon to be, the other for that gloomy art of his by
which he read the hearts of men and saw their doom.

.   .   .   .   .

It has been remarked by many that we mortals are
surrounded by coincidence, and least observe Fate at
its nearest approach, so that friends meet or leave us
unexpectedly, and that the accidents of our lives
make part of a continual play. So it was with these
two. For as they warmly debated, and one of them
had upset and broken his glass while the other lay
back repeating again and again some favourite
phrase, a third was on his way to meet them. A
man much older than either, a man who did nothing
at all and lived when his sister remembered him, was
in that neighbourhood, vaguely wandering and feeling in every pocket for a coin. His hand trembled
with age, and also a little with anxiety, but to his
great joy he felt at last through the lining of his coat
a large round hardness, and very carefully searching
through a tear, and aided by the light that shone
from the windows of " The Lord Benthorpe," he discovered and possessed half a crown. With that he
entered in, for he knew that his friends were there.
In what respect he held them, their accomplish-
ments, and their public fame, I need not say, for

On the Rights of Property

that respect is always paid by the simple to the learned. He sat by them at the little table, drinking also, and for some minutes listened to their stream of affirmation and of vision, but soon he shook his head in a quavering senile way, as he very vaguely caught the drift of their contention. " You've got the wrong end of the stick," he said. . . . " You've got the wrong end of the stick ! . . . Can't take away what a man's got . . . 'tis *wrawng !* . . . 'Vide it up, all the same next week. . . . Same hands ! Same hands !" he went on foolishly wagging his head, and still smiling almost like an imbecile. " All in the same hands again in a week ! . . . 'Vide it up ever so much." They neglected him and continued their ardent debate, and as they flung repeated bolts of theory he, their new companion, still murmured to himself the security of established things and the ancient doctrine of ownership and of law.

But now the night and the stars had come to their appointed hour, and the ending which is decreed of all things had come also to their carousal. A young man of energy stood before them in his shirt sleeves crying, "Time, Time!" as a voice might cry "Doom!" and, by force of crying and of orders, " The Lord Ben thorpe" was emptied, and there was silence at last behind its shutters and its bolted doors.

These three, not yet in a mood for sleep, sauntered together westward through the vast landed estates of London, westward, to their distant homes.

The Economist

A GENTLEMAN possessing some three thousand
acres of land, the most of it contiguous, one
field with another, or, as he himself, his agent, his
bailiff, his wife, his moneylender, and others called
it, "in a ring fence," was in the habit of asking
down to the country at Christmas time some friend
or friends, though more usually a friend than
friends, because the income he received from the
three thousand acres of land had become extremely
small.

He was especially proud of those of his friends who
lived neither by rent from land nor from the proceeds of their business, but by mental activity in
some profession, and of none was he prouder than
of an Economist whom he had known for more than
forty years; for they had been at school together
and later at college. Now this Economist was a
very hearty, large sort of a man, and he made an
amply sufficient income by writing about economics
and by giving economic advice in the abstract to
politicians, and economic lectures and expert economic evidence; in fact, there was no limit to his
earnings except that imposed by time and the
necessity for sleep. He was not married and could

The Economist

spend all his earnings upon himself—which he did.
He was tall, lean, and active, with bright vivacious
eyes and an upstanding manner. He had two sharp
and healthy grey whiskers upon either side of his
face; his hair was also grey but curly; and altogether he was a vigorous fellow. There was nothing
in economic science hidden from him.

This Economist, therefore, and his friend the
Squire (who was a short, fat, and rather doleful man)
were walking over the wet clay land which one of
them owned and on which the other talked. There
was a clinging mist of a very light sort, so that you
could not see more than about a mile. The trees
upon that clay were small and round, and from
their bare branches and twigs the mist clung in
drops; where the bushes were thick and wherever
evergreens afforded leaves, these drops fell with a
patter that sounded almost like rain. There were
no hills in the landscape and the only thing that
broke the roll of the clay of the park land was the
house, which was called a castle; and even this they
could not see without turning round, for they were
walking away from it. But even to look at this
house did not raise the heart, for it was very hideous
and had been much neglected on account of the
lessening revenue from the three thousand acres
of land. Great pieces of plaster had fallen off, nor
had anything been continually repaired except the
windows.

The Economist strode and the Squire plodded on

over the wet grass, and it gave the Squire pleasure
to listen to the things which the Economist said,
though these were quite incomprehensible to him.
They came to a place where, after one had pushed
through a tall bramble hedge and stuck in a very
muddy hidden ditch, one saw before one on the
farther side, screened in everywhere and surrounded
by a belt or frame of low, scraggy trees and stunted
bushes, a large deserted field. In colour it was very
pale green and brown; myriads of dead thistles
stood in it; there were nettles, and, in the damper
hollows, rushes growing. The Economist took this
field and turned his voluble talk upon it. He ap-
preciated that much he said during their walk,
being sometimes of an abstract and always of a
technical nature, had missed the mind of his friend;
he therefore determined upon a concrete instance
and waved his vigorous long arm towards the field
and said :

"Now, take this field, for instance."

"Yes," said the Squire humbly.

"Now, this field," said the Economist, "*of itself*
has no value at all."

"No," said the Squire.

"*That*," said the Economist with increasing earn-
estness, tapping one hand with two fingers of the
other, "that's what the layman must seize first . . .
every error in economics comes from not appreciating that things in themselves have no value. For
instance," he went on, "you would say that a

diamond had value, wouldn't you . . . a large diamond?"

The Squire, hoping to say the right thing, said: "I suppose not."

This annoyed the Economist, who answered a little testily: "I don't know what you mean. What *I* mean is that the diamond has no value in itself. . . ."

"I see," broke in the Squire, with an intelligent look, but the Economist went on rapidly as though he had not spoken:

"It only has a value because it has been transposed in some way from the position where man could not use it to a position where he can. Now, you would say that land could not be transposed, but it can be made from *less* useful to man, *more* useful to man."

The Squire admitted this, and breathed a deep breath.

"Now," said the Economist, waving his arm again at the field, "take this field, for instance."

There it lay, silent and sullen under the mist. There was no noise of animals in the brakes, the dirty boundary stream lay sluggish and dead, and the rank weeds had lost all colour. One could note the parallel belts of rounded earth where once— long, long ago—this field had been ploughed. No other evidence was there of any activity at all, and it looked as though man had not seen it for a hundred years.

On Everything

"Now," said the Economist, "what is the value of this field?"

The Squire had begun his answer, when his friend interrupted him testily. "No, no, no; I don't want to ask about your private affairs; what I mean is, what is it builds up the economic value of this field? It is not the earth itself; it is the use to which man puts it. It is the crops and the produce which he makes it bear and the advantage which it has over other neighbouring fields. It is the *surplus value* which makes it give you a rent. What gives *this* field its value is the competition among the farmers to get it."

"But——" began the Squire.

The Economist with increasing irritation waved him down. "Now, listen," he said; "the worst land has only what is called prairie value."

The Squire would eagerly have asked the meaning of this, for it suggested coin, but he thought he was bound to listen to the remainder of the story.

"That is only true," said the Economist, "of the worst land. There *is* land on which no profit could be made; it neither *makes* nor loses. It is on what we call the *margin of production*."

"What about rates?" said the Squire, looking at that mournful stretch, all closed in and framed with desolation, and suggesting a thousand such others stretching on to the boundaries of a deserted world.

How various are the minds of men! That little word "rates"—it has but five letters; take away the

64

The Economist

" e " and it would have but four—and what different things does it not mean to different men! To one man the pushing on of his shop just past the edge of bankruptcy; to another the bother of writing a silly little cheque; to another the brand of the Accursed Race of our time—the pariahs, the very poor. To this Squire it meant the dreadful business of paying a great large sum out of an income that never sufficed for the bare needs of his life . . . to tell the truth, he always borrowed money for the rates and paid it back out of the next half year . . . he had such a lot of land in hand. Years ago, when farms were falling in, in the eighties, a friend of his, a practical man, who went in for silos and had ɪeen in the Guards and knew a lot about French agriculture, had told him it would pay him to have his land in hand, so when the farms fell in he consoled himself by what the friend had said; but all these years had passed and it had not paid him.

Now to the Economist this little word " rates " suggested the hardest problem—the perhaps insoluble problem—of applied economics in our present society. He turned his vivacious eyes sharply on to the Squire and stepped out back for home, for the Castle. For a little time he said nothing, and the Squire, honestly desiring to continue the conversation, said again as he plodded by his friend's side, "What about rates?"

"Oh, they've nothing to do with it!" said the Economist, a little snappishly. "The proportionate

On Everything

amount of surplus produce demanded by the community does not affect the basic process of production. Of course," he added, in a rather more conciliatory tone, "it *would* if the community demanded the total unearned increment and *then* proposed taxes beyond that limit. *That*, I have always said, would affect the whole nature of production."

"Oh!" said the Squire.

By this time they were nearing the Castle, and it was already dusk; they were silent during the last hundred yards as the great house showed more definitely through the mist, and the Economist could note upon the face of it the coat-of-arms with which he was familiar. They had been those of his host's great-grandfather, a solicitor who had foreclosed. These arms were of stucco. Age and the tempest had made them green, and the head of that animal which represented the family had fallen off.

They went into the house, they drank tea with the rather worried but well-bred hostess of it, and all evening the Squire's thoughts were of his two daughters, who dressed exactly alike in the local town, and whose dresses were not yet paid for, and of his son, whose schooling was paid for, but whose next term was ahead: the Squire was wondering about the extras. Then he remembered suddenly, and as suddenly put out of his mind by an effort of surprising energy in such a man, the date

66

The Economist

February 3rd, on which he must get a renewal or pay a certain claim.

They sat at table; they drank white fizzy wine by way of ritual, but it was bad. The Economist could not distinguish between good wine and bad, and all the while his mind was full of a very bothersome journey to the North, where he was to read a paper to an institute upon "The Reaction of Agricultural Prosperity upon Industrial Demand." He was wondering whether he could get them to change the hour so that he could get back by a train that would put him into London before midnight. And all this cogitation which lay behind the general talk during dinner and after it led him at last to say: "Have you a 'Bradshaw'?"

But the Squire's wife had no "Bradshaw." She did not think they could afford it. However, the eldest daughter remembered an old "Bradshaw" of last August, and brought it, but it was no use to the Economist.

.   .   .   .   .   .

How various is man! How multiplied his experience, his outlook, his conclusions!

A Little Conversation in Carthage   ∽

HANNO : Waiter! Get me a copy of *The Times*.
[*Mutters to himself. The waiter brings the copy*
of The Times. *As he gives it to Hanno he collides*
with another member of the Club, and that member,
already advanced in years, treads upon Hanno's foot.]
HANNO : Ah! Ah! Ah! . . . Oh! [*with a grunt*].
Bethaal, it's you, is it?
BETHAAL : Gouty?
HANNO [*after saying nothing for some time*] : 'Xtra-
ordinary thing. . . . Nothing in the papers.
BETHAAL : Nothing odd about that! [*He laughs*
rather loudly, and Hanno, who wishes he had said the
witty thing, smirks gently without enthusiasm. Then he
proceeds on another track.] I find plenty in the papers!
[*He puffs like a grampus.*]
HANNO : Plenty about yourself! . . . That's the
only good of politics, and precious little good either.
. . . What I can't conceive—as you *do* happen to be
the in's and not the out's—is why you don't send
more men from somewhere ; he has asked for them
often enough.
BETHAAL [*wisely*] : They're all against it; couldn't
get anyone to agree but little Schem [*laughs loudly*];
he'd agree to anything.

A Little Conversation in Carthage

HANNO [*wagging his head sagely*] : He'll be Suffete, my boy! He'll be a Sephad all right! He's my sister's own boy.

BETHAAL [*surlily*]: Shouldn't wonder! All you Hannos get the pickings.

HANNO : You talk like a book. . . . Anyhow, what about the reinforcements ?—that *does* interest me.

BETHAAL [*wearily*] : Oh, really. I've heard about it until I'm tired. It isn't the reinforcements that are wanted really ; it's money, and plenty of it. That's what it is. [*He looks about the room in search for a word.*] That's what it is. [*He continues to look about the room.*] That's what it is . . . er . . . really. [*Having found the word Bethaal is content, and Hanno remains silent for a few minutes, then :*]

HANNO : He doesn't seem to be doing much.

BETHAAL [*jumping up suddenly with surprising vigour for a man of close on seventy, and sticking his hands into his pockets, if Carthaginians had pockets*] : That's it! That's exactly it! That's what I say, What Hannibal really wants is money. He's got the *men* right enough. The *men* are splendid, but all those putrid little Italian towns are asking to be bribed, and I *can't* get the money out of Mohesh.

HANNO [*really interested*]: Yes, now? Mohesh has got the old tradition, and I do believe it's the sound one. Our money is as important to us as our Fleet, I mean our *credit's* as important to us as our Fleet, and he's perfectly right is Mohesh. . . . [*Firmly*]

69

On Everything

I wouldn't let you have a penny if I were at the Treasury.

BETHAAL [*surlily*] : Well, he's bound to take Rome at last anyway, so I don't suppose it matters whether he has the money or not ; but it makes *me* look like a fool. When everything was going well I didn't care, but I do care now. [*He holds up in succession three fat fingers*]. First there was Drephia——

HANNO [*interrupting*] : Trebbia.

BETHAAL : Oh, well, I don't care. . . . Then there was Trasimene ; then there was that other place which wasn't marked on the map, and little Schem found for me in the very week in which I got him on to the Front Bench. You remember his speech ?

[HANNO *shakes his head.*]

BETHAAL [*impatiently*]: Oh well, anyhow you remember Cannae, don't you ?

HANNO : Oh yes, I remember Cannae.

BETHAAL : Well, he's bound to win. He's bound to take the place, and then [*wearily*], then, as poor old Hashuah said at the Guildhall, " Annexation will be inevitable."

HANNO : Now, look here, may I put it to you shortly ?

BETHAAL : [*in great dread*] : All right.

HANNO [*leaning forward in an earnest way, and emphasising what he says*] : All you men who get at the head of a Department only think of the work of that Department. That's why you talk about Hannibal's being bound to win. Of course he's bound to win ;

A Little Conversation in Carthage

but Carthage all hangs together, and if he wins at too great a price in money *you're* weakened, and your *son* is weakened, and *all* of us are weakened. We shall be paying five per cent where we used to pay four. Things don't go in big jumps; they go in gradations, and I do assure you that if you don't send more men——

BETHAAL [*interrupting impatiently*]: Oh, curse all that! One can easily see where *you* were brought up; you smell of Athens like a Don, and you make it worse by living out in the country, reading books and publishing pamphlets and putting people's backs up for nothing. If you'd ever been in politics—I mean, if you hadn't got pilled by three thousand at. . . .

[*At this moment an obese and exceedingly stupid Carthaginian of the name of Matho strolls into the smoking-room of the club, sees the two great men, becomes radiant with a mixture of reverence, admiration, and pride of acquaintance, and makes straight for them.*]

HANNO : Who on earth's that? Know him?

BETHAAL [*in a whisper astonishingly vivacious and angry for so old a man*]: Shut your mouth, can't you? He's the head of my association! He's the Mayor of the town!

MATHO : Room for little un? [*He laughs genially and sits down, obviously wanting an introduction to Hanno.*]

BETHAAL [*nervously*]: I haven't seen you for ages, my dear fellow! I hope Lady Matho's better! [*Turning to Hanno*] Do you know Lady Matho?

On Everything

HANNO [*gruffly*]: Lady *Who?*

BETHAAL [*really angry, and savage on that half of his face which is turned towards Hanno*]: This gentleman's wife!

MATHO [*showing great tact and speaking very rapidly in order to bridge over an unpleasant situation*]: Wonderful chap this Hannibal! Dogged does it! No turning back! Once that man puts his hand to the plough he won't take it off till he's [*tries hard, and fails to remember what a plough does—then suddenly remembering*] till he's finished his furrow. That's where blood tells! Same thing in Tyre, same thing in Sidon, same thing in Tarshish; I don't care who it is, whether it's poor Barca, or that splendid old chap Mohesh, whom they call "Sterling Dick." They've all got the blood in them, and they don't know when they're beaten. Now [*as though he had something important to say which had cost him years of thought*], shall I tell you what I think produces men like Hannibal? I don't think it's the climate, though there's a lot to be said for *that*. And I don't think it's the sea, though there's a lot to be said for *that*. I think it's our old Carthaginian home-life [*triumphantly*]. That's what it is! It isn't even hunting, though there's a lot to be said for that. It's the old—— [*Hanno suddenly gets up and begins walking away.*]

BETHAAL [*leaning forwards to Matho*]: Please don't mind my cousin. You know he's a little odd when he meets anyone for the first time; but he's a really good fellow at heart, and he'll help anyone. But, of

A Little Conversation in Carthage

course [*smiling gently*], he doesn't understand politics any more than—— [*Matho waves his hand to show that he understands.*] But such a good fellow! Do you know Lady Hanno? [*They continue talking, chiefly upon the merits of Hannibal, but also upon their own.*]

The Strange Companion ∾ ∾ ∾

IT was in Lichfield, now some months ago, that I
stood by a wall that flanks the main road there
and overlooks a fine wide pond, in which you may
see the three spires of the Cathedral mirrored.

As I so gazed into the water and noted the clear
reflection of the stonework a man came up beside
me and talked in a very cheery way. He accosted
me with such freedom that he was very evidently
not from Europe, and as there was no insolence in
his freedom he was not a forward Asiatic either;
besides which, his face was that of our own race,
for his nose was short and simple and his lips
reasonably thin. His eyes were full of astonishment and vitality. He was seeing the world. He
was perhaps thirty-five years old.

I would not say that he was a Colonial, because
that word means so little; but he talked English in
that accent commonly called American, yet he
said he was a Brittishur, so what he was remains
concealed; but surely he was not of this land, for,
as you shall presently see, England was more of a
marvel to him than it commonly is to the English.

He asked me, to begin with, the name of the
building upon our left, and I told him it was the

The Strange Companion

Cathedral, to which his immediate answer was, was I sure? How could there be a cathedral in such a little town?

I said that it just was so, and I remembered the difficulty of the explanation and said no more. Then he looked up at the three spires and said: "Wondurful, isn't it?" And I said: "Yes."

Then I said to him that we would go in, and he seemed very willing; so we went towards the Close, and as we went he talked to me about the religion of those who served the Cathedral, and asked if they were Episcopalian, or what. So this also I told him. And when he learnt that what I told him was true of all the other cathedrals, he said heartily: "Is thet so?" And he was silent for half a minute or more.

We came and stood by the west front, and looked up at the height of it, and he was impressed.

He wagged his head at it and said: "Wondurful, isn't it?" And then he added: "Marvlurs how they did things in those old days!" but I told him that much of what he was looking at was new.

In answer to this (for I fear that his honest mind was beginning to be disturbed by doubt), he pointed to the sculptured figures and said that they were old, as one could see by their costumes. And as I thought there might be a quarrel about it, I did not contradict; but I let him go wandering round to the south of it until he came to the figure of a knight with a moustache, gooseberry eyes, and in general a face so astoundingly modern that one did not know what to say or do when one looked at it. It was expressionless.

My companion, who had not told me his name, looked long and thoughtfully at this figure, and then came back, more full of time and of the past of our race than ever; he insisted upon my coming round with him and looking at the image. He told me that we could not do better than that nowadays with all our machinery, and he asked me whether a photograph could be got of it. I told him yes, without doubt, and what was better, perhaps the sculptor had a duplicate, and that we would go and find it this were so, but he paid no attention to these words.

The amount of work in the building profoundly moved this man, and he asked me why there was so much ornament, for he could clearly estimate the vast additional expense of working so much stone that might have been left plain; though I am certain, from what I gathered of his character, he would not have left any building wholly plain, not even a railway station, still less a town hall, but would have had here and there an allegorical figure as of Peace or of Commerce—the figure of an Abstract Idea. Still he was moved by such an excess of useless labour as stood before him. Not that it did not give him pleasure—it gave him great pleasure—but that he thought it enough and more than enough.

We went inside. I saw that he took off his hat, a custom doubtless universal, and, what struck me

76

The Strange Companion

much more, he adopted within the Cathedal a tone
of whisper, not only much lower than his ordinary
voice, but of quite a different quality, and I noticed
that he was less erect as he walked, although his
head was craned upward to look towards the roof.
The stained glass especially pleased him, but there
was much about it he did not understand. I told
him that there could be seen there a copy of the
Gospels of great antiquity which had belonged to
St. Chad; but when I said this he smiled pleasantly,
as though I had offered to show him the saddle of a
Unicorn or the tanned skin of a Hippogriff. Had
we not been in so sacred a place I believe he would
have dug me in the ribs. "St. *Who?*" he whispered,
looking slily sideways at me as he said it. "St.
Chad," I said. "He was the Apostle to Mercia."
But after that I could do no more with him. For
the word "Saint" had put him into fairyland, and
he was not such a fool as to mix up a name like
Chad with one of the Apostles; and Mercia is of
little use to men.

However, there was no quarrelsomeness about
nim, and he peered at the writing curiously, point-
ing out to me that the letters were quite legible,
though he could not make out the words which they
spelled, and very rightly supposed it was a foreign
language. He asked a little suspiciously whether
it was the Gospel, and accepted the assurance that
it was; so that his mind, sceptical to excess in some
matters, found its balance by a ready credence in

others and remained sane and whole. He was again touched by the glass in the Lady Chapel, and noted that it was of a different colour to the other and paler, so that he liked it less. I told him it was Spanish, and this apparently explained the matter to him, for he changed his face at once and began to give me the reason of its inferiority.

He had not been in Spain, but he had evidently read much about the country, which was moribund. He pointed out to me the unnatural attitude of the figures in this glass, and contrasted its half-tones with the full-blooded colours of the modern work behind us, and he was particularly careful to note the irregularity of the lettering and the dates in this glass compared with the other which had so greatly struck him. I was interested in his fixed convictions relative to the Spaniards, but just as I was about to question him further upon that race I began to have my doubts whether the glass were not French. It was plainly later than the Reformation, and I should have guessed the end of the sixteenth or beginning of the seventeenth century. But I hid the misgiving in my heart, lest the little trust in me which my companion still had should vanish altogether.

We went out of the great building slowly, and he repeatedly turned to look back up it, and to admire the proportions. He asked me the exact height of the central spire, and as I could not tell him this I felt ashamed, but he told me he would find it in a book, and I assured him this could be

done with ease. The visit had impressed him
deeply; it may be he had not seen such things
before, or it may be that he was more at leisure to
attend to the details which had been presented to
him. This last I gathered on his telling me, as we
walked towards the Inn, that he had had no work
to do for two days, but that same evening he was to
meet a man in Birmingham, by whom, he earnestly
assured me, he was offered opportunities of wealth
in return for so small an investment of capital as
was negligible, and here he would have permitted
me also to share in this distant venture, had I not,
at some great risk to that human esteem without
which we none of us can live, given him clearly to
understand that his generosity was waste of time,
and that for the reason that there was no money to
invest. It impressed him much more sharply than
any plea of judgment or of other investments could
have done.

Though I had lost very heavily by permitting
myself such a confession to him, he was ready to
dine with me at the Inn before taking his train, and
as he dined he told me at some length the name of
his native place, which was, oddly enough, that of a
great German statesman, whether Bismarck or another I cannot now remember; its habits and its
character he also told me, but as I forgot to press
him as to its latitude or longitude to this day I am
totally ignorant of the quarter of the globe in which
it may lie.

On Everything

During our meal it disturbed him to see a bottle of wine upon the table, but he was careful to assure me that when he was travelling he did not object to the habits of others, and that he would not for one moment forbid the use in his presence of a beverage which in his native place (he did not omit to repeat) would be as little tolerated as any other open temptation to crime. It was a wine called St. Emilion, but it no more came from that Sub-Prefecture than it did from the hot fields of Barsac; it was common Algerian wine, watered down, and—if you believe me—three shillings a bottle.

I lost my companion at nine, and I have never seen him since, but he is surely still alive somewhere, ready, and happy, and hearty, and noting all the things of this multiple world, and judging them with a hearty common sense, which for so many well fills the place of mere learning.

The Visitor   ⌒ ⌒ ⌒ ⌒ ⌒

AS I was going across Waterloo Bridge the other
day, and when I had got to the other side of
it, there appeared quite suddenly, I cannot say
whence, a most extraordinary man.

He was dressed in black silk, he had a sort of
coat, or rather shirt, of black silk, with ample
sleeves which were tied at either wrist tightly with
brilliant golden threads. This shirt, or coat, came
down to his knees, and appeared to be seamless.
His trousers, which were very full and baggy, were
caught at his ankles by similar golden threads. His
feet were bare save for a pair of sandals. He had
nothing upon his head, which was close cropped.
His face was clean shaven. The only thing approaching an ornament, besides the golden threads
of which I have spoken, was an enormous many-
coloured and complicated coat-of-arms embroidered
upon his breast, and showing up magnificently
against the black.

He had appeared so suddenly that I almost ran
into him, and he said to me breathlessly, and with a
very strong nasal twang, "Can you talk English?"

I said that I could do so with fluency, and he
appeared greatly relieved. Then he added, with

6   81

that violent nasal twang again, "You take me out of this!"

There was a shut taxi-cab passing and we got into it, and when he had got out of the crush, where several people had already stopped to stare at him, he lay back, panting a little, as though he had been running. The taxi-man looked in sud denly through the window, and asked, in the tone of voice of a man much insulted, where he was to drive to, adding that he didn't want to go far.

I suggested the "Angel" at Islington, which I had never seen. The machine began to buzz, and we shot northward.

The stranger pulled himself together, and said in that irritating accent of his which I have already mentioned twice, "Now say, *you*, what year's this anyway?"

I said it was 1909 (for it happened this year), to which he answered thoughtfully, "Well, I have missed it!"

"Missed what?" said I.

"Why, 1903," said he.

And thereupon he told me a very extraordinary but very interesting tale.

It seems (according to him) that his name was Baron Hogg; that his place of living is (or rather will be) on Harting Hill, above Petersfield, where he has (or rather will have) a large house. But the really interesting thing in all that he told me was this: that he was born in the year 2183,

The Visitor

"which," he added lucidly enough, "would be your 2187."

"Why?" said I, bewildered, when he told me this.

"Good Lord!" he answered, quite frankly astonished, "you must know, even in 1909, that the calendar is four years out?"

I answered that a little handful of learned men knew this, but that we had not changed our reckoning for various practical reasons. To which he replied, leaning forward with a learned, interested look:

"Well, I came to learn things, and I lay I'm learning."

He next went on to tell me that he had laid a bet with another man that he would "hit" 1903, on the 15th of June, and that the other man had laid a bet that he would get nearer. They were to meet at the Savoy Hotel at noon on the 30th, and to compare notes; and whichever had won was to pay the other a set of Records, for it seems they were both Antiquarians.

All this was Greek to me (as I daresay it is to you) until he pulled out of his pocket a thing like a watch, and noted that the dial was set at 1909. Whereupon he began tapping it and cursing in the name of a number of Saints familiar to us all.

It seems that to go backwards in time, according to him, was an art easily achieved towards the middle of the Twenty-second Century, and it was

worked by the simplest of instruments. I asked
him if he had read "The Time Machine." He
said impatiently, "You have," and went on to
explain the little dial.

"They cost a deal of money, but then," he added,
with beautiful simplicity, "I have told you that I
am Baron Hogg."

Rich people played at it apparently as ours do at
ballooning, and with the same uncertainty.

I asked him whether he could get forward into
the future. He simply said : "What *do* you mean ? "

"Why," said I, "according to St. Thomas, time
is a dimension, just like space."

When I said the words "St. Thomas" he made a
curious sign, like a man saluting. "Yes," he said
gravely and reverently, "but you know well the
future is forbidden to men." He then made a
digression to ask if St. Thomas was read in 1909.
I told him to what extent, and by whom. He got
intensely interested. He looked right up into my
face, and began making gestures with his hands.

"Now that really *is* interesting," he said.

I asked him "Why ? "

"Well, you see," he said in an off-hand way,
"there's the usual historic quarrel. On the face of it
one would say he wasn't read at all, looking up the
old Records, and so on. Then some Specialist gets
hold of all the mentions of him in the early Twentieth Century, and writes a book to show that even
the politicians had heard of him. Then there is a

discussion, and nothing comes of it. *That's* where the fun of Travelling Back comes in. You find out."

I asked him if he had ever gone to the other centuries. He said, " No, but Pop did." I learned later that " Pop " was his father.

" You see," he added respectfully, " Pop's only just dead, and, of course, I couldn't afford it on my allowance. Pop," he went on, rather proudly, " got himself back into the Thirteenth Century during a walk in Kent with a friend, and found himself in the middle of a horrible great river. He was saved just before the time was up."

" How do you mean ' the time was up ' ? " said I.

" Why," he answered me, " you don't suppose Pop could afford more than one hour, do you? Why, the Pope couldn't afford more than six hours, even after they voted him a subsidy from Africa, and Pop was rich enough, Lord knows! Richer'n I am, coz of the gurls. . . . I told you I was Baron Hogg," he went on, without affectation.

" Yes " said I, " you did."

" Well, now, to go back to St. Thomas," he began——

" Why on earth——? " said I.

He interrupted me. " Now that *is* interesting," he said. " You know about St. Thomas, and you can tell me about the people who know about him, but it *does* show that he had gone out in the Twentieth Century, for you to talk like that! Why, I got full marks in St. Thomas. Only thing I did

85

get full marks in," he said gloomily, looking out of the window. " That's what *counts*," he added: "none of yer high-falutin' dodgy fellows. When the Colonel said, ' Who's got the most stuff in him ? ' (not because of the rocks nor because I'm Baron Hogg), they all said, ' *That's* him.' And that was because I got first in St. Thomas."

To say that I simply could not make head or tail of this would be to say too little : and my muddlement got worse when he added, " That's why the Colonel made me Alderman, and now I go to Paris by right."

Just at that moment the taxi-man put in his head at the window and said, with an aggrieved look :

" Why didn't you tell me where I was going ? "

I looked out, and saw that I was in a desolate place near the River Lea, among marshes and chimneys and the poor. There was a rotten-looking shed close by, and a policeman, uncommonly suspicious. My friend got quite excited. He pointed to the policeman and said :

" Oh, how like the pictures ! Is it true that they are the Secret Power in England ? Now *do*—— "

The taxi-man got quite angry, and pointed out to me that his cab was not a caravan. He further informed me that it had been my business to tell him the way to the " Angel." His asset was that if he dropped me there I would be in a bad way ; mine was that if I paid him off there he would be in a worse one. We bargained and quarrelled, and as

The Visitor

we did so the policeman majestically moved up, estimated the comparative wealth of the three people concerned, and falsely imagining my friend to be an actor in broad daylight, he took the taxi-man's part, and ordered us off back to the "Angel," telling us we ought to be thankful to be let off so lightly. He further gave the taxi-man elaborate instructions for reaching the place.

As I had no desire to get to the "Angel" really, I implored the taxi-man to take me back to Westminster, which he was willing to do, and on the way the Man from the Future was most entertaining. He spotted the public-houses as we passed, and asked me, as a piece of solid, practical information, whether wine, beer, and spirits were sold in them. I said, "Of course," but he told me that there was a great controversy in his generation, some people maintaining that the number of them was, in fiction, drawn by enemies; others said that they were, as a fact, quite few and unimportant in London, and others again that they simply did not exist but were the creations of social satire. He asked me to point him out the houses of Brill and Ferguson, who, it seems, were in the eyes of the Twenty-second Century the principal authors of our time. When I answered that I had never heard of them he said, "That *is* interesting." I was a little annoyed and asked him whether he had ever heard of Kipling Miss Fowler, or Swinburne.

He said of course he had read Kipling and Swin-

On Everything

burne, and though he had not read Miss Fowler's
works he had been advised to. But he said that
Brill for wit and Ferguson for economic analysis
were surely the glories of our England. Then he
suddenly added, "Well, I'm not sure about 1909.
The first *Collected* Brill is always thought to be 1911.
But Ferguson! Why he knew a lot of people as
early as 1907! He did the essay on Mediæval
Economics which is the appendix to our school text
of St. Thomas.

At this moment we were going down Whitehall.
He jumped up excitedly, pointed at the Duke of
Cambridge's statue and said, "That's Charles I."
Then he pointed to the left and said, "That's the
Duke of Buccleuigh's house." And then as he saw
the Victoria Tower he shouted, "Oh, that's Big Ben,
I know it. And oh, I say," he went on, "just look
at the Abbey!" "Now," he said, with genuine
bonhomie as the taxi drew up with a jerk, "are
those statues symbolic?"

"No," I said, "they are real people."

At this he was immensely pleased, and said that
he had always said so.

The taxi-man looked in again and asked with
genuine pathos where we really wanted to go to.

But just as I was about to answer him two powerful men in billycock hats took my friend quietly but
firmly out of the cab, linked their arms in his, and
begged me to follow them. I paid the taxi and
did so.

The Visitor

The strange man did not resist. He smiled rather foolishly. They hailed a four-wheeler, and we all got in together. We drove about half a mile to the south of Westminster Bridge, stopped at a large Georgian house, and there we all got out. I noticed that the two men treated the stranger with immense respect, but with considerable authority. He, poor fellow, waved his hand at me, and said with a faint smile as he went through the door, arm in arm with his captors:

"Sorry you had to pay. Came away without my salary ticket. Very silly." And he disappeared.

The other man remaining behind said to me very seriously, "I hope his Lordship didn't trouble you, sir?"

I said that on the contrary he had behaved like an English gentleman, all except the clothes.

"Well," said the keeper, "he's not properly a Lord as you may say; he's an Australian gent. But he's a Lord in a manner of speaking, because Parliament did make him one. As for the clothes—ah! you may well ask! But we durstn't say anything: the doctor and the nurse says it soothes him since his money trouble. But *I* say, *make* 'em act sensible and they will be sensible."

He then watched to see whether I would give him money for no particular reason, and as I made no gestures to that effect I went away, and thus avoided what politicians call "studied insolence."

A Reconstruction of the Past ～ ～

" IT has been said with some justice that we know
more about the Victorian Period in England
than we do of any one of the intervening nine centuries, even of those which lie closest to our own
time, and even of such events as have taken place
upon our own soil in the Malay Peninsula. I will
attempt to put before you very briefly, as a sort of
introduction to the series of lectures which I am
to deliver, a picture of what one glimpse of life in
London towards the end of the Nineteenth Century
must have resembled.

" It is a sound rule in history to accept none but
positive evidence and to depend especially upon the
evidence of documents. I will not debate how far
tradition should be admitted into the reconstruction
of the past. It *may* contain elements of truth; it
must contain elements of falsehood, and on that
account I propose neither to deny nor to admit this
species of information, but merely to ignore it; and
I think the student will see before I have done with
my subject that, using only the positive information
before us, a picture may be drawn so fully detailed
as almost to rival our experience of contemporary
events.

A Reconstruction of the Past

"We will imagine ourselves," continued the professor, with baleful smile of playful pedantry, "in Piccadilly, the fashionable promenade of the city, at nine o'clock in the morning, the hour when the greatest energies of this imperial people were apparent in their outdoor life ; for, as we know from the famous passage which we owe to the pen of the pseudo-Kingsley, the English people, as befitted their position, were the earliest risers of their time. We will further imagine (to give verisimilitude to the scene) the presence of a north-east wind, in which these hardy Northerners took exceptional delight, and to which the anonymous author above alluded to has preserved a famous hymn.

"Piccadilly is thronged with the three classes into which we know the population to have been divided—the upper class, the middle, and the lower, to use the very simple analytical terms which were most common in that lucid and strenuous period. The lower class are to be seen hurrying eastward in their cloth caps and 'fustian,' a textile fabric the exact nature of which is under dispute, but which we can guess, from the relics of contemporary evidence in France, to have been of a vivid blue, highly glazed, and worn as a sort of sleeved tunic reaching to the knees. The head-gear these myriads are wearing is uniform : it is a brown skull cap with a leather peak projecting over the eyes, the conjectural 'cricket cap,' of which several examples are preserved. It has been argued by more than one

authority that the article in question was not a
headgear. It appears in none of the statuary of the
period. No mention of it is made in any of the vast
compilations of legal matter which have come down
to us, and attempts have been made to explain in an
allegorical sense the very definite allusions to it with
which English letters of that time abound.   I am
content to accept the documentary evidence in the
plain meaning of the words used, and to portray to
you these 'toiling millions' (to use the phrase of
the great classic poet) hurrying eastward upon this
delightful morning in March of the year 1899
Each is carrying the implement of his trade (possession in which was secured to him by law). The one
holds a pickaxe, another balances upon his head a
ladder, a third is rolling before him a large square
box or 'trunk'—a word of Oriental origin—upon a
'trolley' or small two-wheeled vehicle dedicated to
some one of the five combinations of letters which
had a connection not hitherto established with the
system of roads and railways in the country.   Yet
another drags after him a small dynamo mounted on
wheels, such as may be seen in the frieze illustrating
the Paris Exhibition of ten years before.

"Interspersed with this crowd may be seen the
soldiery, clad entirely in bright red.   But these, by
a custom which has already the force of law, are
compelled to occupy the middle of the thoroughfare.
They are of the same class as the labouring men
round them, and like these carry the implements of

A Reconstruction of the Past

their trade, with which we must imagine them from time to time threatening the passers-by. All, I say, are hurrying eastward to their respective avocations in the working part of this great hive.

"Appearing as rarer units we perceive members of the second or *middle* class proceeding at a more leisurely and dignified pace towards their professional or commercial pursuits, the haunts of which lie less to the eastward and more in the centre of the city. These are dressed entirely in black, and wear upon their heads the round hat to which one of my colleagues erroneously gave the title of a religious emblem, a position from which, I am glad to see, he has recently receded. Nothing is more striking in the scene than the absolute uniformity of this costume. In the right hand is carried, according to the ritual of a secret society to which the greater part of this class belong, a staff or tube. The left hand grasps a roll of printed paper which we may premise without too much phantasy to be the original news-sheet from which the innumerable forgeries and copies of the succeeding dark ages proceeded. We are, of course, ignorant of its name, but we may accept it as the prototype of that vast mass of printed matter which purports to be contemporary in date, but which recent scholarship has definitely proved to be of far later origin. Beyond these, but in numbers certainly few, the exact extent of which I shall discuss in a moment, are the *upper* classes, or Gentry. How many they may

On Everything

be in such a crowd, I repeat, we cannot tell.
We know that to the whole population they stood
somewhat as one to 10,000. The proportion in
London may have been slightly higher, for we
have definite documentary information that in certain provincial centres 'not a gentleman' could be
discovered, though for what reason these centres
were less favoured we are not told. In a street
full of some thousands we shall certainly not be
exaggerating if we put the number of the Gentry
present at certainly a couple of individuals, and
we may put as our highest limits half a dozen.
How are they dressed? In a most varied manner.
Some in grey, some in pink (these are off to hunt
the fox in the fields of Croydon or upon the heath
of Hampstead, or possibly—to follow the conjecture
of the Professor of Geology in his fascinating book
on the Thames Valley—to Barking Level). Others
are in black silk with a large oval orifice exposing
the chest. Others again will be in white flannel,
and others in a species of toga known as 'shorts.'
These are students from the university, or their
professors, and they will be distinguished by a square
cap upon the head which, unlike so many other
conjectural forms of headgear, we can definitely
pronounce to have had a religious character. A
tassel sometimes of gold hangs from the centre of
this square. With the exception of this headgear
the Gentry discover upon their heads as uniform
a type of covering as their inferiors of the middle

class, who salute them as they pass by lifting the round hat with the right hand. This headgear is tubular and probably of some light metal, polished to a highly reflecting surface, and invariably (as we know by the fascinating diaries recently collected by the University Press) polished in the same direction upon some sort of lathe.

"If we are lucky we may see at this hour one member of a class restricted even among the few gentlemen of that period, the Peers. Should we see such an one he will be walking in a red plush robe. It is probable that he will carry upon his head the same species of hat as the others of his rank, but I admit that it is open to debate whether this hat were not surrounded by a circle of metal spikes, each surmounted with a small ball. Such a person will be walking at an even more leisurely pace than the few other members of the Gentry who may be present, and upon the accoutrements of his person will be discovered a small shield, varying in size from a couple of inches to as many feet, stamped with a representation of animals and often ornamented by a device in the English or in the Latin tongue. These devices, many of which have come down to us engraved upon metal, are of the utmost value to the historian. They have enabled him to reconstruct the exact appearance of animals now long extinct, and it is even possible in some cases to ascertain the particular families to which they belonged. No class of object, however, has suffered more from frequent forgeries than these emblems. Luckily there is an almost invariable test for recognising such forgeries, which consists in the use of the French language misspelt. Of some thousands of such signs many hundreds affect a legend in the French tongue, and of these hardly one is correctly spelt. Moreover, essential words are often omitted, and in general the forgeries betray that imperfect acquaintance with the con‹ temporary language of Paris which was one of tht marks of social inferiority at that time. When I add that the total number of Peers at any given moment was less than seven hundred out of forty million people, while the number of these shields which have been discovered already amounts to over five hundred thousand, it will be apparent that the proportion of genuine emblems must be very small. Now and then a house will bear the picture of some such shield painted and hung out upon a board before it. This sometimes, but not universally, indicates the nobility of the tenant. In the mattei of religion . . ." At this point the professor looked narrowly at his notes, held one sheet of them in various positions, put it up to the light, shook his head, and next, observing the hour, said that he would deal with this important subject upon the following Wednesday or Thursday, according to sale of tickets during the intervening days. With these words after a fit of coughing, he withdrew

The Reasonable Press

IT is difficult to repress a feeling of natural indigna-
tion when one considers the policy which the
Government and Mr. Robespierre have seen fit to
pursue during the last two years, and especially since
the unfortunate blunder of Mr. Danton and Mr.
Desmoulins. We have never hidden our opinion that
these two gentlemen—able and disinterested men as
they undoubtedly were—acted rashly in stepping out
of the party (as it were) and attempting to form an
independent organisation at a moment when the
strictest discipline was necessary in the face of the
enormous and servile majority commanded by the
Government. However unrepresentative that majority may be of the national temper at this moment, the
business of a member of the Convention lies chiefly
on the floor of the House, and it is the height of un-
wisdom to divide our forces even by an act of too
generous an enthusiasm for the cause. We would
not write a word that might give offence to the surviving relatives of the two statesmen we have named,
but this much *must* be said : the genius of the nation
is opposed to particular action of this sort; the

electors understand Government and Opposition, by separate action like Mr. Danton's and Mr. Desmoulin's they are simply bewildered. Such eccentric displays do no good, and may do very great harm. Meanwhile, we must repeat that the general attitude of the Government is indefensible. That is a strong word, but hardly too strong under the circumstances. It is not the executions themselves which have (as we maintain) alienated public sentiment, nor their number—though it must be admitted that 1200 in four months is a high record—it is rather the pressure of business in the Courts and the disorganisation of procedure which the Plain Man in the Street notices and very rightly condemns, and we would warn Mr. Robespierre that unless a larger number of judges are created under his new Bill the popular discontent may grow to an extent he little imagines, and show itself vigorously at the polls. We are all agreed that Mr. Carnot shows admirable tact and energy at the War Office, and it is characteristic of that strong man that he has left to others the more showy trappings of power. We would urge upon him as one who is, in a sense, above party politics, to counsel his colleagues in the Government in the direction we have suggested. It may seem a small point, but it is one of practical importance, and the Man in the Street cares more for practical details than he does for political theories.

The Reasonable Press

The present moment is opportune for reviewing the work of the Government to date, and drawing up a political balance-sheet as it were of its successes and failures. We have always been open critics of the present Administration, whenever we thought that national interests demanded such criticism, and our readers will remember that we heartily condemned the ill-fated proposal to change the place of public executions from the Place de la Revolution to the Square de l'Egalité—a far less convenient spot; but apart from a few tactical errors of this sort it must be admitted, and is admitted even by his enemies, that Mr. Robespierre has handled a very difficult situation with admirable patience and with a tremendous grasp of detail. It is sometimes said of Mr. Robespierre that he owes his great position mainly to his mastery over words. To our thinking that judgment is as superficial as it is unjust. True, Mr. Robespierre is a great orator, even (which is higher praise) a great *Parliamentary* orator, but it is not this one of his many talents which is chiefly responsible for his success. It is rather his minute acquaintance with the whole of his subject which impresses the House. No assembly in the world is a better judge of character than the Convention, and its appreciation of Mr. Robespierre's character is that it is above all a practical one. His conduct of the war—for in a sense the head of the Government and

99

On Everything

Leader of the House may be said to conduct any and every national enterprise — has been remarkable. The unhappy struggle is now rapidly drawing to a close and we shall soon emerge into a settlement to which may be peculiarly applied the phrase "Peace with Honour." The restraint and kindliness of our soldiers has won universal praise, even from the enemy, and it is a gratifying feature in the situation that those of our fellow-citizens in Toulon, Lyons, and elsewhere who could not see eye to eye with us in our foreign and domestic policy are now reconciled to both. One last word upon the Judges Bill. We implore Mr. Robespierre to stand firm and not to increase the present number, which is ample for the work of the Courts even under the somewhat exceptional strain of the last four years. After all it is no more fatigue to condemn sixty people to death than one. The delay in forensic procedure is (or rather was) due to its intolerable intricacy, and the reforms introduced by Mr. Robespierre himself, notably the suppression of so-called "witnesses" and of the old-fashioned rigmarole of "defence," has done wonders in the way of expedition. We too often forget that Mr. Robespierre is not only a consummate orator and a past master of prose, but a great lawyer as well. We should be the last to hint that the demand for more judges was due to place-hunting : vices of that kind are happily absent in France whatever may be the case in other countries. The real danger is rather that if the new posts were created jealousy

The Reasonable Press

and a suspicion of jobbery might arise *after* they
were filled. Surely it is better to leave things as
they are.

THE OPPOSITION PAPER : LOBBY NOTES

Really the Government Press seems determined to
misrepresent last Friday's incident! Mr. Talma has
already explained that his allusion to cripples was
purely metaphorical and in no way intended for
Mr. Couthon, for whom, like everyone in the House,
he has the highest respect.

THE GOVERNMENT PAPER : LOBBY NOTES

Last Friday's incident is happily over. Mr. Talma
has assured Mr. Couthon that he used the word
"cripple" in a sense quite different from that in
which that highly-deservedly popular gentleman
unfortunately took it.

SOCIAL AND PERSONAL

The Marquis de Misenscene is leaving Paris to-
night for Baden Baden. His Lordship intends to
travel in the simplest fashion and hopes his incognito
may be preserved.

Mr. Couthon, the deservedly popular M.P., made a
pathetic sight yesterday at Mr. Robespierre's party
in the Tuileries Gardens. As most people know, the
honourable gentleman has lost the use of his lower

limbs and is wheeled about in a bath-chair, but he can still gesticulate freely and his bright smile charms all who meet him.

Madame Talma was At Home yesterday on behalf of the Society for the Aid and Rescue of Criminal Orphans. Whatever our political differences we all can unite in this excellent work, and the great rooms of Talma House were crowded. At Madame Talma's dinner before the reception were present Major Bonaparte, Mr. Barrere, Mr. St. Just, Mrs. Danton (widow of statesman), Mrs. Desmoulins (mother of the late well-known author-journalist), and Miss Charlotte Robespierre, who looked charming in old black silk with a high bodice and jet trimmings.

LETTERS TO THE PAPERS

Sir,—I hope you will find space in your columns for a protest against the disgraceful condition of the public prisons. I have not a word to say, sir, against the presence of the prisoners in such large numbers at this exceptional moment; moreover, as nearly all their cases are *sub judice* it would be highly improper in me to comment upon them. I refer, sir, only to the intolerable noise proceeding from the cells and rendering life a burden to all ratepayers in the vicinity. Prisoners are notoriously degenerate and often hysterical, and the nuisance created by their lamentations and protests is really past bearing. I can assure the Government that if they do not provide gags, *and use them,* they shall certainly not have my vote at the next election.—I am, &c.,

DISGUSTED.

Sir,—*May* I trespass upon your space to make known to our *many* friends that the memorial service for my late husband, the Archbishop of Paris, is postponed till the 1st Decadi in Fructidor?—With many thanks in advance for your courtesy, I am, &c.,

ASPASIA GOREL.

OFFICIAL NEWS

We are requested by the Home Office to give publicity to the arrangements for to-morrow's executions. These will be found on page 3. There will be no executions on the day after to-morrow.

" CAN you not show me," said the Student, as they flew swiftly through the upper air over Madrid, he clinging tightly to the Devil's skirts, " can you not show me other sights equally entertaining before we finish our journey ? "

" Readily," replied Asmodeus, " for I have the power of showing you every heart and thought in Madrid, and of unroofing every house if it be my pleasure, and I am determined to repay you in whatever way you choose for the service you have done me. First, then, cast your eyes down at the very well-dressed gentleman whom you see in that open taxi-cab, enjoying as he whirls along the warm air of a night in the season. He is a wealthy man in charge of one of the great departments of State ; nay, I can tell you which one, for the mines in Peru are his special department."

" Doubtless," said the Student, " he is at this moment considering some weighty matter in connection with his duties."

" No," said the Devil ; " you must guess again."

" Why, then, since you have shown me so many diverting weaknesses in men I must believe that he is plotting for the advancement of some favourite."

Asmodeus

"Yet again you are wrong," said the Devil. "His whole mind is occupied in watching the sums marked by the taximeter, which he constantly consults by the aid of a match; only last Wednesday, the Feast of St. Theresa, he was overcharged a matter of a quarter of a real by one of these machines, and he is determined this shall not happen again. You perceive the great house which he is now passing. It is lit up at every window, and the sounds of music are proceeding from it."

"I not only see it," said the Student, "but have seen this sort of sight so often during the season in Madrid that I am certain you will not find anything here to surprise me."

"No," said the Devil, "I was perhaps wrong in attempting to amuse you by so commonplace a spectacle as that of a moneylender entertaining very nearly all those in Madrid with whom he has had no dealings, and even some of those who are in his power; that is, if, on account of their nobility or from some other cause, it is worth his while to have them seen in his rooms. But what I would particularly point out to you is, not this kind of feast which (as you say) you have seen a thousand times, but the old man who is mumbling strange prayers over a dish of food in that common servants' room which you may perceive to lie half above the ground and half beneath it next to the kitchen. He is the father of the wealthy gentleman who is entertaining the guests upstairs."

On Everything

"It is evident," said the Student, "that he has no liking for High Life."

"No," said Asmodeus, "and in this eccentricity he is supported with true filial sympathy by his son."

"I perceive," said the Student, "a man tossing uneasily in his sleep, and from time to time crying out as one does to a horse when it is restive, or rather as men cry to horses which they can hardly control."

"I am well acquainted with him," said the Devil. "He is one of my most earnest clients, but in nothing does he divert me more than in these nightmares of his wherein he cries 'Whoa there! Steady, old girl!' And again, 'Now then! Now then!' not omitting from time to time, 'You damned brute!' and a cuff upon his pillow."

"To what, my dear Asmodeus, do we owe this diversion?" asked the Student wonderingly. "He seems to be a wealthy man, if we may judge by the house in which we see him and the furniture of the room in which he so painfully sleeps. And surely there is nothing upon his mind?"

"You are wrong," said the Devil; "there is upon his mind a most weighty matter, for he considers it a necessity in his position to ride every morning along the soft road especially prepared for that exercise upon the banks of the Manzanares, where he may meet the wealth and fashion of Madrid occupied in the same pastime. But unfortunately for him he is wholly devoid of the art of equitation and stands in as much terror of his mount as does a lady of her dressmaker. For one hour, therefore, of every day, he suffers such tortures that I greatly fear we shall not be able to add to them appreciably in my dominions when the proper time arrives. But let us leave these wealthy people, whose foibles are, after all, much the same, and turn to the poorer quarters which lie south of the King's Royal Palace."

In a few moments they had reached these and were examining a mean house not far from the Church of St. Alphonso, in a bare upper room of which a woman with a starved and anxious expression was writing, late as was the hour, at top speed

" Poor woman ! " said the Student. " I perceive that she is one of those unhappy people whom grinding poverty compels to produce ephemeral literature which is afterwards printed and sold at one real for the divertisement of the populace of Madrid. I know of no trade more pitiful, and I can assure you the sight of her industry moves me to the bottom of my heart."

" The sight is indeed pitiful," said the Devil, " to those at least who permit themselves the luxury of pity—a habit which I confess I have long ago abandoned. For you must know that in the company of Belphegor, Ashtaroth, and the rest even the softest-hearted of devils will grow callous. But more interesting to you perhaps than the sad necessities of her trade is the matter which she is at present engaged upon."

" What is that ? " said the Student.

" Why," said Asmodeus, " she is writing ' Nellie's Notes' for a paper called *The Spanish Noblewoman*, and she is at this very moment setting down her opinion that there is no better way to pass a rainy afternoon than taking out and cleaning one's Indian Bracelets, Ropes of Pearls, Diamonds, and other gems. She is good enough to add that she herself thinks it wise and a good discipline to clean her own jewellery and not leave it to a maid."

" In the room below you will see a young man whom 1 very much regret to say is in a state of complete intoxication."

" I do not know," said the Student, " why you should regret such a sight, for I had imagined that all human frailty was a matter of pleasure to your highnesses."

" Yes," replied Asmodeus, " in the general it is so, but you must know that this particular vice is so inimical to the province which I control that I regard it with peculiar detestation, and I am not upon so much as speaking terms with Shamarel, who has been deputed by the Council to look after those who exceed in wine."

" Is not that the same," asked the Student, " whom they say twice appeared to a hermit at Carinena ? "

" You are right," said Asmodeus, betraying a

slight annoyance, "but pray do not put it about that a personage of such importance was at the pains of appearing to a common hermit. The fact is, he was at that moment visiting the Campo Romano to assure himself that the vines were in good condition, and it was by the merest accident that the hermit caught sight of him during this journey, for you must know that he makes it a punctilio never to appear in person to one under the rank of Archbishop, and even then he prefers that the recipient of the favour should be a Cardinal into the bargain, and if possible a Grandee of Spain."

"You have told me so much about your amiable colleague," said the Student, "that you have forgotten to tell me whether any moral divertisement attached to the poor young fellow whom we see in that offensive stupor."

"No," said the Devil, "now I come to think of it, there is perhaps nothing remarkable in his condition, unless you think it worthy of notice that he is a medical student and will shortly be entrusted with the nerves and veins of the poor in the public hospitals of Madrid. It is to be hoped that he will soon put behind him these youthful follies, for if he persists in them they will make his hand tremble, and in that case he will never be permitted to practise the art of surgery upon the persons of the wealthy and more remunerative classes."

"Outside the house," said the Student, "I see a

policeman walking with some solemnity, and I confess that the sight is pleasing to me, for it gives me
a feeling that the good people of Madrid are well
looked after when so expensive an instrument of
the law is spared for so poor a quarter."

"You are right," said Asmodeus, "and were I
now to show you the inner heart of the Duke of
Medina y Barò who controls the police forces of
Madrid, you would find that his chief anxiety in the
distribution of his men came from the dilemma
in which he perpetually finds himself, whether to
furnish them rather in large numbers to the
wealthier quarters for the defence of which police-
men exist, or for the poorer quarters, the terrorising
of which is necessarily their function."

"At any rate," said the Student, "he need not
bother himself about the houses of that large
number of people (and I am one) from whom there
is nothing to steal and who yet have never learnt
any of the arts of theft. In a word, he is spared
the trouble either of protecting or of keeping down
what are called the middle classes."

"True," said Asmodeus, "but most unfortunately
this kind of person does not herd together in special
districts. If they did so it would be a great relief
to the strain upon the Police Department; but they
are scattered more or less evenly throughout the
wealthier and the poorer quarters."

"Can you tell me," asked the Student, "whether
it is worth our while to watch the policeman for a

few moments in the exercise of his duties and whether he would provide us with any entertainment as we watched him unseen?"

"Alas!" answered the Devil sadly, "I have no power to forecast the future; but from my knowledge of the past I can tell you that during the ten years since he has joined the force this officer has not once arrested a rich man in error on a dark night, nor perjured himself before a Magistrate so openly as to be detected, nor done any of those things which legitimately amuse us in people of his kind."

"But do you not think," said the Student, "that we might by remaining here see him help an old woman across the road amid the plaudits of the governing classes, or take a little child that is lost by the hand and lead it to its mother's home?"

"Doubtless," said the Devil, yawning, "we should find him up to tricks of that sort were we willing to wait here, floating in the air, for another ten or dozen hours, when the streets will be full of people. But the play-acting to which you so feelingly allude is but rarely indulged in by these gallant men when onlookers are wanting. Come, the sky is already pale in the direction of the eastern mountains; it will soon be day, and I desire before you are completely tired out to show you one more sight."

With these words Asmodeus took the Student by the hand and darted with inconceivable rapidity over the roofs of the city until he came to a particular spot which he had evidently marked in his flight.

"Cast your eyes," he said, "upon this narrow but busy thoroughfare beneath us. It is the only street in Madrid which at so late an hour is still full of people and of business. It is called Fleet Street."

"I have heard of it," said the Student.

"No doubt," said the Devil; "but what I particularly desire to point out to you is a man whom you will see in his shirt-sleeves, seated upon a swivel-chair and writing away for dear life, matter which will appear to-morrow in the *Morning Post.*"

"Well," said the Student, "what of that?"

"Can you guess what he is writing?" asked Asmodeus.

"That I am quite unable to do," said the Student.

"It is," said the Devil, "a series of satirical remarks upon the frailties and follies of others—and yet he is a journalist!'

The Death of the Comic Author 〜 〜

A COMIC Author of deserved repute was lodging at the beginning of this month in a house with broken windows, in a court off the Gray's Inn Road.

He had undertaken to produce a piece of Humorous Fiction to the length of 75,000 words.

The Comic Author, a man of experience (for this was his forty-seventh book), had sat down to begin his task. He calculated how long it would last him. He was good for 1500 words a day, if they were short words, and even when doom or accident compelled him to the use of long ones he could manage from 1163 to 1247.

The specification was lucid and simple. There was to be nothing in the work that could offend the tenderness of the patriot nor the ease of good manners, let alone the canons of decency and right living. A powerful love interest which he was compelled under Clause VII of his contract to introduce immediately after each of the wittiest passages had been deftly woven into the fabric, and (as was clearly laid down in Clause IX) no matter already published might appear in those virgin pages. If any did so, be sure it was so veiled by the tranposition of phrases and other slight changes of manner as to escape the publisher's eye.

So far so good. But upon the 13th of August, a day of great beauty, but of excessive heat, the Comic Author, sitting at his desk, was struck by Apollo, the God and patron of literary men.

It was the custom of the Comic Author, who was a teetotaler and a vegetarian, to wear a soft shirt entirely made of wool and devoid of a collar, which ornament, he was assured by Members of the Faculty, exercised a prejudicial effect upon the health. It was equally his custom to compose his famous periods with his back turned to the light. This habit he had also adopted at the dictation of the Faculty, who had proved to him beyond possibility of refutation that the human eye is damaged by nothing more than by reading or writing with one's face towards the window. With his back, therefore, to the window in his room (it was unbroken), it was the Comic Artist's wont to sit at a plain and dirty small deal table and express his mind upon paper, his head reposing upon his left hand, his fountain pen grasped firmly in his right, and his lips and tongue following the movement of his nib as it slowly crawled over the page before him.

The Comic Author (again under the impulse of the Faculty) kept his hair cut short at the back ; to cut it short all over was more than his profession would allow. You have, then, the Comic Author sitting at his desk with his back to the unbroken window, his neck exposed from the shortness of hair and the absence of collar, under the brilliant light of the 13th of August.

A fourth condition must now be considered : by some physical action never properly explained, glass, though it may act as a screen to radiant heat, will also store and intensify the action of sunlight. So that anything placed immediately beneath it upon a bright day will (it is notorious) suffer or enjoy an effect of heat far greater than that discoverable upon its outer side. The common greenhouse is a proof of this. The Comic Author was therefore in a situation to receive the full power of Apollo. It took the form of a sunstroke, and with his story uncompleted, nay, in the midst of an unfinished phrase, he fell helpless.

His Landlady, summoning a neighbour to her aid (for the charwoman never stayed after ten o'clock, and it was already noon), dragged him to his room and sent for the parish doctor, who, after a brief examination of the patient, declared him to be in some danger; but the poor fellow was not so far gone as to forget his obligations, and he murmured a few words which, after some difficulty, they understood to be the address of the publisher whom he would not for worlds have disappointed. Imagining this address to be in some way connected with a pecuniary advantage to herself, the Landlady sent to it immediate word of his accident, and within half an hour a motor-car of surpassing brilliance and immense power was purring at the door. From this vehicle descended in a gentlemanly but commanding manner One who seemed far too great for the humble lodging which he entered. And the Doctor, leaving his patient for a moment, was pleased to receive the visitor in a lower room, while the Landlady, who was also interested in the event, listened with due courtesy in the passage without.

The Publisher (for it was he) learned with increasing concern the desperate position of the Comic Author, and while he was naturally chiefly concerned with the financial loss the little accident might involve, it should be remembered to his credit that he made inquiries as to the state of the patient and even asked whether he suffered physical pain. Upon hearing that the Comic Author, though fuddled by cerebral congestion, did undoubtedly suffer the Visitor's brow perceptibly darkened ; he pointed out to the Doctor that if this accident had but happened ten days later it would have had consequences much less serious to himself.

The Doctor was eager to point out that the fault was none of his. He had come the moment he had heard of the case, and, moreover, sunstroke was a disease which betrayed itself by no premonitory symptoms. He assured the Publisher that if the Comic Author's survival could in any way be of service to the firm he would do everything in his power to save his life.

The Publisher replied, a little testily, that the value of the Comic Author's survival would entirely

The Death of the Comic Author

depend upon the talent remaining to him after his recovery, and pointed out what the Doctor had overlooked, that a sensational death, if it received due recognition from the Press, often caused the works of the deceased to sell for a week or more with exceptional rapidity.

He next asked whether the Comic Author had not left manuscripts, and the Landlady was pleased to bring him not only all that lay upon the deal table, but much more beside, and all his private correspondence as well, which she found where she had often perused it, in various receptacles of her lodger's room.

The Publisher upon receiving these seemed to feel his position less acutely, and sending the sheets out at once to his secretary in the car (with instructions that those stories or sketches hitherto unpublished should be carefully noted) he resumed his conversation with the medical man. He was first careful to ask how long cases of this sort when they proved fatal commonly endured, and expressed some relief at hearing that certain benignant exceptions had lingered for several days. He was further assured that lucid intervals might be counted on, and in general he discovered that the lines upon which the story had been intended to proceed might be recovered from the lips of the dying man before he should exchange the warm and active existence of this world for the Unknown Beyond.

He re-entered his motor-car, therefore, with a

much lighter heart, promising to send an Expert
Stenographer who should take down the last and
necessary instructions from the lips of Genius. The
motor-car then left that court off the Gray's Inn
Road where the tragedy was in progress, and swept
westward to the larger atmosphere of St. James's.

At this point again, when the activity and decision
of one master brain seemed to have saved all, Fate
intervened. The Expert Stenographer, having lacked
regular employment for nearly eighteen weeks, was
so overjoyed at learning the news and the price attached to his immediate services, that he could not
resist cheerful refreshment and conversation with
friends in celebration of the occasion. He reached
the Gray's Inn Road, therefore, somewhat late in the
day; he was further delayed by a difficulty in dis-
covering the house with broken windows which had
been indicated to him, and when he entered it was
to receive the unwelcome news that the Comic
Author was dead.

The Doctor, whose duties had already for some
hours called him to other scenes where it was his
blessed mission to alleviate human suffering, was not
present to confirm the sad event, and the Expert
Stenographer, who could not believe that he had
been baulked of so unexpected a piece of fortune,
insisted upon proof which the Landlady was unable
to afford. He even sat for some few moments by
the side of the Poor Lifeless Clay in the vain hope
that some further indication as to the general trend

The Death of the Comic Author

of the book might fall from the now nescient lips. But they were dumb.

How many consequent misfortunes depended upon this untoward accident the reader may easily guess. The Landlady, to whom the Comic Author had owed thirty shillings for a month's rent and service, was in a very natural anxiety for some days, an anxiety which was increased by the discovery that her former lodger had no friends, while his few relatives seemed each to have, in their own small way, claims against him of a pecuniary nature.

His dress clothes, upon which she had confidently counted, turned out to belong to a costumier of the neighbourhood, who loudly complained that he had had no notice of this intempestive demise, and was at least a sovereign out of pocket by so awkward a conjunction; nor was he appreciably relieved when it was pointed out to him that the suit would at least carry no contagious disease.

The Stenographer, as I have already indicated, lost the remuneration dependent upon his Expert Services, and was further at the charge of the refreshment which he had foolishly consumed in anticipation of that gain.

The Doctor, indeed, was not disappointed, for he had expected nothing, but by far the worst case was that of the generous and wealthy man who had been at all the risk of advertising, partly printing, and already ordering the binding of the work which he now found himself at a loss to produce.

On Everything

There is no moral to this simple story : it is one
of the many tragedies which daily occur in this great
city, and from what I know of the Comic Author's
character, he would have been the last to have in-
flicted so much discomfort had it in any way depended
upon his own volition ; but these things are beyond
human ordinance.

On certain Manners and Customs   ∽   ∽

I WAS greatly interested in the method of government which I discovered to obtain in the Empire of Monomotapa during my last visit there. I say "during my last visit" because although, as everyone knows, I have repeatedly travelled in the more distant provinces of that State, I had never spent any time to speak of in the capital until I delayed there last month for the purpose of visiting a friend of mine who is one of the State Assessors. He was good enough to explain to me many details of their Constitution which I had not yet grasped, and I conceive it—now that I have a full comprehension of it—to be as wise a method of governing as it is a successful one.

I must first put before the reader the elements of the matter. Every citizen in Monomotapa takes a certain fixed rank in the State; for the inhabitants of that genial clime have at once too much common sense and too strict a training to talk nonsense about equality or any other similar metaphysical whimsey. Every man, therefore, can precisely tell where he stands in relation to his fellows, and all those heart-burnings and jealousies which are the bane of other States are by this simple method at

once exorcised. Moreover, the method by which
a man's exact place is determined is simplicity itself,
for it reposes upon his yearly revenue; and there is
a gradually ascending scale from the poorest, whose
revenue may not amount from all sources to more
than 40 Tepas a month, to the Supreme Council, the
wealthier members of which may have as much as
10,000,000 Tepas a month, or even more. There is
but one drawback to this admirably practical and
straightforward way of ordering the State, which is
that by a very ancient article of their religion the
Monomotapians are each forbidden to disclose to
others what the state of their fortunes may be. It
is the height of impertinence in any man, even a
brother, to put questions upon the matter; all documents illuminating it are kept strictly secret, and
though religious vows and binding oaths are very
much disliked among this people, yet one is rigidly
observed, which is that forbidding the divulgence by
a bank of the sums of money entrusted to it by its
clients. Certain rash spirits have indeed proposed
to destroy the anomaly and either to make some
other standard arrange the order of society (which
is unthinkable) or else to allow questions of money
to be freely debated, and the incomes of all to be
matter of public comment.

Now, like many excellent and rational attempts
at religious or social reform, these propositions must
wholly fail in practice. As for setting up some
other standard than that of wealth by which to

decide the importance of one's fellow citizens, the Monomotapians very properly regard such a proposal as fantastic to the point of buffoonery. Nor, to do them justice, do those who propose the scheme seriously intend this part of it. They rather put it forward to emphasise the second half of their programme, which has much more to be said for it. But here a difficulty arises of a sort that often upsets the calculations of idealists, namely, that however much you change the laws you can with more difficulty change the customs of the people, and though you might compel all banking accounts to be audited, or even insist upon every man making a public return of his income, yet it is certain that the general opinion upon this matter would result, in practice, in much the same state of affairs as they now have. Men would devise some other system than that of banks; their returns would be false, and there would be a sort of general unconscious conspiracy among all to support fraud in this matter.

My host next explained to me the manner in which laws are made among the Monomotapians and the manner in which they are administered. It seems that by a fundamental rule of their Constitution no law may be passed in less than twenty-five years, unless it can be proved to have its origin in terror.

If indeed those who are the wealthiest and therefore the most important in the State can prove to the satisfaction of all that they have gone blind with panic, then indeed the passage of a law is permitted even in a few hours. Thus, when a certain number of young gentlemen had so far forgotten their good breeding as to torture by way of sport considerable numbers of the poorer classes, one of these in his turn, oblivious to the rules of polite behaviour, so far forgot himself as to strike his young master in the face. It was under these circumstances, when the greater part of the governing classes had fled abroad, or were closely locked in behind their doors, that the "Tortures Restrictions Bill" was passed; but this haste was even then regarded as somewhat indecent, and it would have been thought more honourable to have discussed the matter for at least two days. Nominally, however, affairs of real importance cannot be legislated upon, as I have said, in less than twenty-five years. It is customary for the Monomotapians first to wait until some neighbouring State has attempted a particular reform. When that reform has been working for some years, if it be successful in its working, the wealthier Monomotapians begin to talk about it according to set rules. And it is again a fundamental point in their Constitution that one-half of those who so debate must be for, the other half against the proposed change. The discussion is carried on by some seventy or eighty men, of whom two-thirds at least must possess a fortune of at least 1000 Tepas a month, but it is customary to mix among them one or two men of exceptional poverty,

On certain Manners and Customs

as this is imagined in some way or other to please the Gods. The middle class, on account of their intolerable habit of referring to learned books and to the results of their travel, are very properly excluded. These, then, debate for a term of years, and when they are weary of it they will very often begin to debate again. Meanwhile the institution or the reform upon which their discussion has turned will have taken root in those foreign countries which it is their pride to copy, and they can at last be certain that in following suit Monomotapa will have nothing to lose. When all this is decided a certain number of men are set apart, the poorer of whom are given a sum of money and the wealthier certain titles on condition that they vote in favour of the change ; while another body of men are set apart and rewarded in a precisely similar manner for giving a pledge of the opposite sort. But great care is taken that the first body shall be slightly larger than the second, for by an unexplained decision of their priests the force of a law depends upon the margin between the two bodies so chosen. These electors once named are put into an exceedingly narrow passage in which it would be difficult for any very stout person to move at all. At the end of the passage doors still narrower open upon the street, the door upon the left being used to record affirmative, that upon the right negative votes. The whole mass, which consists of near a thousand men, is then kindly but firmly pushed

by Assistants of the King (as they are called) until
its last member has been squeezed through one of
the two doors. This process is immensely popular
among the Monomotapians, who will gather in
crowds to cheer the wretched men whom avarice or
ambition has devoted to so pleasant a task. And
when they have come out, covered with sweat and
perhaps permanently affected in their hearts by the
ordeal, they are very often granted civic honours
by their fellow-townsmen over and above the sums
of money or titles which they have already received.
With such frenzied delight do the Monomotapians
regard this singular practice that even women have
lately petitioned to be permitted to join in the
scrimmage. This they will undoubtedly be granted
in cases where they can prove a certain wealth, for,
indeed, there is no reason why an exercise of this
sort should be confined to one sex. But it is understood that a certain part of the women of Monomotapia, many of them also wealthy, are willing to
pay money to prevent such a result, and if this
indeed be the case a very curious situation, almost
unknown in the annals of Monomotapia, will arise ;
for since all government is in the hands of the rich,
it is necessary that the rich should act together in
serious affairs of State. And what on earth will
happen when one section of the wealthy, whether
men or women, are opposed to the actions of
another section, it would indeed be difficult to determine. Nor are the older men and the more

On certain Manners and Customs

experienced without grave misgivings as to the issue of such an unprecedented conflict.

I cannot conclude without telling you briefly the manner in which their Kings are elected, for it reflects in every detail at once the originality and the wisdom of this people.

There are in Monomotapa some three or four hundred public halls in which is conducted the national sport, which consists in competitions between well-known talkers as to who can talk the longest without exhaustion, and it rapidly becomes known, through well-developed agencies of information as well as by public repute, which individuals have attained to the greatest proficiency in this regard. Sometimes in the remotest province will arise a particular star, but more often it is in the Metropolis or its neighbourhood that your really great talkers can be found ; a man in the tradition of that great King of the last century who upon one occasion talked the clock round and was in reward for that feat permitted to hold the Kingship for three terms in succession.

When by a process of elimination the two strongest talkers have been discovered, they are brought to the capital, set up upon a stage before a vast audience of Assessors (of which my friend, as I have told you, was one), and begin talking one against the other with great rapidity, starting at a signal made by an official who is paid for this duty a very high salary indeed. It may well be imagined that the interest in the struggle grows keen after the first few hours have passed. The panting breath, the discoloured cheeks, the drooping attitude of either competitor, call forth cheers of encouragement from his supporters and even murmurs of sympathy from his numerous judges. At last, it may be in the sixth or the seventh hour, one of the two goes groggy—if I may so express myself—he falters in his words, perhaps repeats himself, passes his hand to his forehead or takes a drink of gin (which, from its resemblance to water, is greatly favoured in these contests). Such signals of distress are the beginning of the end. His successful rival, straining himself to one last effort, will pour out a great string of sentences of an approved pattern, dealing as a rule with the glories and virtues of those who have listened to him, of their ancestry, and their hold upon the Monomotapian State, and as the defeated competitor falls lifeless to the floor this successful fellow is crowned amid the applause of the vast assembly. I was at the pains to ask whether it was necessary that these long harangues should make sense, for it seemed to me that this added labour would very materially handicap many men who might otherwise possess all the physical requirements of victory, and I was free to add that it would seem to me, at least, as a foreigner, very foolish to weigh down some fine athlete worthy of the Crown by demanding of him the rare characteristics of the pedant. I was relieved to hear that there was no obligation as to the choice of words used or the order in which they were to be pronounced, saving that they must be words in the vulgar tongue. But it seems, oddly enough, that the trainers in this sport after generations of experience have discovered that the competitors actually suffer less fatigue if they will repeat certain set and ritual phrases than if they take refuge in mere gibberish, just as men marching in step are said to suffer less fatigue than men marching at ease. So at least I was assured, but my insufficient acquaintance with the Monomotapian tongue forbade me to make certain upon the matter.

The Statesman   ◇   ◇   ◇   ◇

"HÔTEL DE FERRAS, PARIS, *August* 1, 1846.

" MY dear Father,—I got in here last night, after
a very painful and tiresome journey, at eleven
o'clock. At least it was eleven o'clock by Calais
time, but they are so careless in this country about
their clocks that it would be very difficult to say
what the right time really was were I not able to
consult the excellent chronometer which you and
Mamma were so kind as to give me after my success
in the Schools at Oxford this summer. I confess to
the childishness of having rung the chimes in it five
or six times during the night to while away the
tedium of the journey in the Diligence from Beauvais. Beauvais contains a really remarkable cathedral, but it is unfinished. I notice, indeed, that
many of the buildings undertaken by the French
remain in an incomplete condition. The Louvre,
for instance (which is so near this hotel, and the
roofs of which I can see from my window), would be
a really fine building if it were completed, but this
has never been done, and the total effect is very
distressing. I fancy it is the numerous wars, in
which the unhappy people have been engaged at
the caprice of their rulers, which have led to such

deplorable inconsequence. You have often warned me not to judge rashly upon a first impression, but I confess the people seem to me terribly poverty-stricken, especially in the country districts, where the children may often be seen hobbling about in rough *wooden* shoes, without stockings to their feet. I say no more. I hope, dear Papa, that when Parliament meets I shall be returned from Italy, and that I shall be able to follow your action in the House of Commons. You know how ardently I attend to the great struggle for Free Trade, to the attainment of which, as of every form of Righteousness, you have ever trained my early endeavours.

"I am, your affectionate son,

"Jo. Bilsted."

"Hôtel de Ferras, *January* 15, 1853.

"My dear Julia,—I write you a hurried note to tell you that I have left behind me, at Number Eleven, my *second beaver hat.* It is in the hatbox in the white cupboard on the landing outside the nursery door. Do not send anything else with it, as you were imprudent enough to do last time I asked you to despatch luggage ; the Customs are very particular, and it is important for me just now, amid all these political troubles, not to have what the French call 'histoires.' I have really nothing to tell you more as to the condition of affairs, nor anything to add to the brief remarks in my last letter. Were I not connected by business ties with

the Continent nothing should tempt me to this kind
of journey again. The train service is ridiculously
slow, and there is a feeling of distress and ill-ease
wherever one goes. It is truly amazing to me that
any people, however stunted by centuries of oppres-
sion, should tolerate the form of government which
has been recently set up by brute force in this unhappy country! Meanwhile, though everyone dis
cusses politics, nothing is *done*, and the practical
things of life are wholly neglected. The streets
still remain the narrow, ill-lit thoroughfares which
would be a disgrace to a small English provincial
town, and the Army, so far as any civilian can
judge, is worthless. The men slouch about with
their hands in their pockets; the Cavalry sit their
horses very badly; and even the escort of the
'Emperor' would look supremely ridiculous in any
other surroundings. I have little doubt that if
horse-racing were more thoroughly developed the
Equine Race would improve. As it is, the horses
here are deplorable. I hope to persuade M. Behrens,
who is one of the few sensible and clear-sighted men
I have met during this visit, to accept our proposals,
and I will write you further on the matter.

"Your affectionate husband,
"Jo. BILSTED.

"P.S.—I somewhat regret that you have accepted
the invitation to the Children's Party. However,
I never interfere with you in these matters. I must,

however, positively forbid your taking little Charles, who, though he is eldest, suffers, I fear, from a weak heart, inherited from your dear mother. I hope to return this day fortnight."

"HÔTEL DE FERRAS, *July* 15, 1870.

"My dear Julia,—It was a matter of great regret to me that you should have been compelled to leave Paris a few days before myself; but I shall follow to-morrow, and hope to be at Number Eleven by Thursday at the latest. You will then have learned the terrible truth that war has been finally declared. Nothing could have more deeply *im*pressed and *op*pressed me at the same time. The overwhelming military power which in better hands and under a proper guidance might have been turned to such noble uses is to be hurled against the insecure combination of German States which have recently been struggling, perfectly rightly in my opinion, to become One Great Nation; for I make no doubt that the lesser States will throw in their lot with Prussia: a menace to one is a menace to all. I write from the bottom of my heart (my dear Julia), when I say that I am convinced that after the first triumphs of this Man of Blood our own Government will speak with no uncertain voice, and will defend the new German people against the aggressor. It was sufficiently intolerable that his Italian policy should have been framed before our eyes, without intervention, and that the unity of that ancient land should be deferred through his insolence. I have not borne to visit Rome since the hateful presence of a foreign garrison was established there. I will even go so far (perhaps against your own better judgment) as to raise the matter in Parliament, but I greatly fear that the House will not be sitting when the most drastic action is needed. However, I repeat what I have said ; I am confident in the ultimate Righteousness of our intervention. I am therefore confident that we shall not allow the further expansion of this Military Policy.

"As I write the garish, over-lit façades of this luxurious Babylon, its broad, straight streets, with their monotonous vulgar splendour, and the swarms of the military all round, fill me with foreboding. It would be a terrible thing if this very negation of True Civilisation and Religion were to triumph, and I am certain that unless we speak boldly we ourselves shall be the next victim. But we *shall* speak boldly. . . . My faith is firm.

"Your affectionate husband,

"Jo. Bilsted.

"P.S.—I am glad that Charles has got through his examination successfully. I hope he clearly understands that I have no intention of letting him be returned for Pensbury until a year has elapsed."

"Hôtel de Ferras, *April* 1, 1886.

"My dear Charles,—It was a filial thought in you to send a letter which would reach me upon my sixtieth birthday, and believe me that, speaking as your father, I am not insensible to it.

"I wish you could come and see your mother and me if only for a few hours, but I know that your Parliamentary duties are heavier than ever; indeed, life in the House of Commons is not what it used to be! In my time it was often called 'the best club in Europe.' Alas, no one can say that now! Meanwhile your mother and I are very happy pottering about our old haunts in Paris; but you have no idea, my dear Charles, how changed it all is! You can, of course, remember the Second Empire as a child, but to your mother and me, who were so intimate with Paris during its most brilliant period, there is something tragic in the sight of this great capital since the awful chastisement of fifteen years ago. We ought not, of course, to judge foreign nations too harshly, but after no inconsiderable experience of Parliamentary life I cannot but have the most gloomy forebodings as to the future of this nation. There seems no settled policy of any kind. Yesterday I attended a debate in the Chamber, but the various speakers articulated so rapidly that I was not able to follow them with any precision. It is surely an error to pour out torrents of words in this fashion, and I cannot believe there is any mature thought behind it at all. I regret to say that the practice of duelling, though denounced by all the best thought in the country, is still rife, and nowhere do occasions for its exercise arise more frequently

than in the undisciplined political life of this capital.
One must not, however, look only on the dark side ;
there are certainly some very fine new buildings
springing up, especially in the American quarter
towards the Arc de Triomphe. Of course your
mother and I keep to the old Hôtel de Ferras. We
are at an age now when one does not easily change
one's habits, but it seems to me positively dingy
compared with some of these new great palaces.
It is a comfort, however, to deal with people who
know what an English banknote is, and who will
take an English cheque, and who can address one
properly on the outside of an envelope. It amused
your dear mother to see how quickly they seized the
new honour which her Majesty has so graciously
conferred upon me.

" Your affectionate father,

" Jo. Bilsted."

" Hôtel de Ferras, October 19, 1906.

" My dear Charles,—I cannot tell you how warmly
I agree with your last letter upon the state of
Europe. I am an old man, I have seen many men
and things, and I have been particularly familiar with
foreign policy ever since I first entered the House
of Commons, now nearly fifty years ago, but rarely
have I known a moment more critical than the present. My one comfort lies in the fact that in spite
of the divisions of Party, the heart of the nation
is still sound, and the leaven of common sense in

the electors will save us yet. I feel a shade of regret sometimes to think that the division no longer retains its old name; I should like to feel that, father and son, we had held it for three generations, but though the name has changed, the spirit of the place is the same. . . . I beg you to mark my words; I may say without boasting that I have rarely been wrong in my judgment of foreign affairs. When one sees things here one sometimes trembles for the future.

"This Hotel is not at all what it was. It is ill-kept and damp, and I shall not return to it.

"Expect me in London before the end of the week.
                                        "PENSHURST."

[Lord Penshurst died shortly after his return to London. He was succeeded by his son Charles, second Baron, but the Division is still represented by a member of the family in the person of Mr. George Bilstead, his second son, the husband of Mrs. Bilstead, and author of *The Coming Struggle in the Balkans.*]

The Duel ⌒　⌒　⌒　⌒　⌒　⌒

IN the year 1895 of blessed memory there was
living in the town of Paris at the expense of his
parents a young English gentleman of the name of
Bilbury; at least, if that were not his name his
name was so nearly that that it doesn't matter. He
spoke French very well, and had for his age (which
was twenty-four) a very good working acquaintance
with French customs. He was popular among the
students with whom he associated, and it was his
especial desire not to seem too much of a foreigner
on the various occasions when French life contrasts
somewhat with that of this island. It was something of a little mania of his, for though he was
patriotic to a degree when English history or English
habits were challenged, yet it made him intolerably
nervous to feel exceptional or eccentric in the town
where he lived. It was upon this account that he
fought a duel.

There happened to be resident in the town of
Paris at the same time another gentleman, whose
name was Newman ; he also was young, he also was
English, but whereas Mr. Bilbury was by genius
a painter, Mr. Newman was by vocation an engineer.
And while Mr. Bilbury would spend hours in the

The Duel

studio of a master whom (in common with the other
students) he despised, Mr. Newman was continually
occupied in playing billiards with his fellow students
of engineering in the University. And while Mr.
Bilbury was spending quite twelve hours a day in
finding out how to make a picture look like a thing
if you stood a long way off from it (which is the end
and object of his school in Paris), Mr. Newman had
already acquired the art of making a billiard ball
come right back again towards the cue after it had
struck its neighbour. Mr. Bilbury had learned how
to sing in chorus with the other students songs relating in no way to pictorial excellence; Mr. Newman had learned to sing those songs peculiar to
students of engineering, but relating in no way to
applied physics. In a word, these two young gentlemen had never met.

But one day Mr. Bilbury, going arm-in-arm with
three friends towards the river, met upon the pave-
ment of the Rue Bonaparte Mr. Newman in much
the same posture, but accompanied by a rather
larger bodyguard. It would have been astonishing
to anyone little acquainted with the temper of students in the University, and indeed it *was* astonishing
both to Mr. Newman and to Mr. Bilbury, though
they had now for some months been acquainted
with the inhabitants of that strange corner of the
universe, to see how this trifling incident provoked
an altercation which in its turn degenerated into a
vulgar quarrel. Each party refused to give way to

139

the other, and the members of each began compar-
ing the members of the other to animals of every
kind such as the pig, the cow, and even certain
denizens of the deep.   In the midst of the hubbub
Mr. Bilbury, not to be outdone in the racy vigour of
youth, shouted at Mr. Newman (who for all he
knew might have been a Russian revolutionary or
a man from St. Cyr) an epithet which he had
come across in the contemporary literature of the
capital, and which he imagined to be of common
exchange among the merry souls of the University.
To his surprise—nay, to his alarm—a dead silence followed the use of this very humble and ordinary word.
Mr. Newman, to whom it was addressed, was not indeed
ignorant of its meaning (for it meant nothing in
particular and was offensive), but was astonished
at the gravity of those round him when the little
epithet had been uttered.   With a sense of surprise
now far exceeding that of Mr. Bilbury he saw his
companions draw themselves up stiffly, take off their
eccentric felt hats with large sweeping gestures,
and march him off as stiff as pokers, leaving the
Bilbury group solemn with the solemnity of men
who have a duty to perform.

That duty was very quickly accomplished.   The
eldest and most responsible of the three friends told
Bilbury very gently but very firmly that there could
be no issue but one to the scene which had just
passed.

" I am not blaming you, my dear John." he said

The Duel

kindly (Mr. Bilbury's name was John), "but you know there can be only one issue."

Meanwhile Mr. Newman's friends, after maintaining their strict and haughty parade almost the whole length of the Rue Bonaparte, broke silence together, and said : "It is shameful, and you will not tolerate it!" To which Mr. Newman replied by an assurance that he would in no way fall beneath the dignity of the situation.

More than this neither Mr. Bilbury nor Mr. Newman knew, but they both went to bed that night much later than either intended, and each felt in himself a something of what Ruth felt when she stood among the alien corn, or words to that effect.

And next morning each of them woke with the knowledge that he had some terrible business on hand with some ass of a foreigner who had got excited, or, to be more accurate, had suddenly stopped being excited for wholly incomprehensible reasons at a particular moment in a lively conversation. Both Mr. Newman and Mr. Bilbury were, I say, in this mood when there entered to Mr. Newman in his room in the Rue des Ecoles (which he could ill afford) two of his friends of the night before, who said to him very simply and rapidly that it would be better for them to act as his seconds as the others had chosen them as most fitted. To this Mr. Newman murmured his adhesion, and was about to ask anxiously whether he would soon see them again, when with a solemnity quite out of keeping with their usual good-fellowship, they bowed in a ritual manner and disappeared.

Meanwhile a similar scene was taking place in the little fourth-floor room which Mr. Bilbury occupied, and Mr. Bilbury, somewhat better acquainted with the customs of the University, dismissed his two friends with a little speech and awaited developments.

Before lunch the thing was arranged, and Mr. Newman, who was waiting in a rather hopeless way for his friends' return, was informed at about twelve o'clock that all was settled; it was to be at the end of the week, up in Meudon, in a field which belonged to one of his friends' uncles. " We are less likely to be disturbed there," said the friend, "and we can carry the affair to a satisfactory finish." Then he added : " It has a high wall all round it."

" But," said the other second, interrupting him, " since we have chosen pistols that will not be much good, for the report will be heard."

" No," said the first second in a nonchalant manner, " my uncle keeps a shooting gallery and the neighbours will think it a very ordinary sound. You had," he explained courteously to Mr. Newman, " the choice of weapons as the insulted party, and we chose pistols of course."

" Of course," said Mr. Newman, who was not going to give himself away upon details of this kind.

" The other man's seconds," went on Mr. Newman's friend genially, " wanted swords, but we told them that you couldn't fence; besides which, with amateurs nothing ever happens with swords. And then," he continued, musing, "if the other man is really good you're done for, whereas with pistols there is always a chance."

To Mr. Bilbury, equally waiting for the luncheon hour in some gloominess of soul, the same tale was told, *mutatis mutandis,* as they say in what is left of the classical school of the University. His adversary had chosen pistols. "And you know," said one of his seconds to Bilbury sympathetically, "he had the right of choice; technically he was the insulted party. Besides which, pistols are always better if people don't know each other."

The other second agreed, and was firmly of the opinion that swords were only for intimate friends or politicians. They also mentioned the field at Meudon, but with this difference that it became in their mouths the ancient feudal property of one of their set, and they were careful to point out that the neighbours were all Royalists, devotedly attached to the family, and the safest and most silent wit. nesses in the world."

For the remaining days Mr. Bilbury and Mr. Newman were conducted by their separate groups of friends, the first to a shooting gallery near Vincennes, the second to a shooting gallery near St. Denis. Their experiments were thus conducted many miles apart: and it was just as well. It was remarkable what an affluence of students came as

the days proceeded to see the exercise in martial
sport of Mr. Newman. At first from fifty to sixty
of the students with one or two of the pure mathe-
maticians and three or four chemists comprised the
audience, but before the week was over one might
say that nearly all the Applied Physics and Positive
Sciences of the University were crowding round
Vincennes and urging Mr. Newman to accurate and
yet more accurate efforts at the target. At St. Denis
the number of artists increased in a similar proportion, and to these, before the week was ended,
were added great crowds of poets, rhetoricians, and
even mere symbolists, who wore purple ties and
wigs. These also urged Mr. Bilbury to add to his
proficiency; and sometimes that principal himself
would shudder to see a long-haired and apparently
inept person with a greenish face pick up a pistol
with dreadful carelessness and put out the flame of
a candle at a prodigious distance with unerring aim.

When the great day arrived two processions of
such magnitude as gave proof of the latent wealth
of the Republic crawled up the hill to Meudon. The
occasion was far too solemn for a trot, and two men
at least of those present thought several times un-
comfortably about funerals. I must add in connection
with funerals that a large coffin was placed upon
trestles in a very conspicuous part of the field, into
which each party entered by opposite wooden gates
which, with the high square wall all round, quite
shut out the surrounding neighbourhood. The two

groups of friends (each over a hundred in number
all dressed in black and most of them in top-hats,
retired to opposite corners of the field, nor was there
any sign of levity in either body in spite of their
youth; the four seconds, who were in frock-coats and
full of an unnatural importance, deposited upon the
ground between them a very valuable leather case
which, when it was opened, discovered two perfectly
new pistols of a length of barrel inordinate even for
the use of Arabs, let alone for civilised men. These
two were loaded in private and handed to either
combatant, and Mr. Bilbury and Mr. Newman, having
been directed each to hold the pistol pointed to the
ground, were set apart by either wall while the
seconds proceeded to pace the terrain. Mr. Newman
remembered the cricket pitches of his dear home
which perhaps he would never see again ; Mr. Bilbury
could think of nothing but a tune which ran in his
head and caused him grave discomfort.

When the ceremony of the pacing was over the
two unfortunate gentlemen were put facing each
other, but twisted, with the right side of the one
turning to the corresponding side of the other, so as to
afford the smallest target for the deadly missiles ; and
then one of the seconds who held the handkerchief
retired to some little distance to give the signal.

It was at this juncture, as Mr. Newman and Mr.
Bilbury stood with their pistols elevated towards
heaven, and waiting for the handkerchief to drop,
each concentrated with a violent concentration upon

the emotions of the moment, that a prodigious noise of hammering and shouting was heard at one of the doors of the enclosure, and that three gentlemen— the one wearing a large three-coloured sash, the like of which neither Mr. Bilbury nor Mr. Newman had ever seen—entered and ordered the whole party to desist in the name of the law. So summoned, the audience with the utmost precipitation climbed over the wall, forced itself through the gates, and in every manner at its disposal vanished. And the gentleman with the tri-coloured sash, sitting down in the calmest manner upon one of the trestles and turning the coffin over by way of making a table, declared himself a public officer, and took notes of all that had occurred. It was interesting to see the businesslike way in which the seconds gave evidence, and the courtesy with which the two principals were treated as distinguished foreigners by the gentleman with the three-coloured sash. He was young, like all the rest, amazingly young for a public official of such importance, but collected and evidently most efficient. When he had done taking his notes he stood up in a half-military fashion, ranged Mr. Newman and Mr. Bilbury before him, and very rapidly read out a series of legal sentences, at the conclusion of which was a fine of one hundred francs apiece, and no more said about the matter. Mr. Bilbury and Mr. Newman were astonished that attempted homicide should cost so little in this singular country. They were still more astonished to discover that etiquette

The Duel

demanded a genial reconciliation of the two com-
batants under such circumstances, and they were
positively amazed to find after that reconciliation
that they were compatriots.

It was their seconds who insisted upon standing
the dinner that evening. The whole incident was
very happily over save for one passing qualm which
Mr. Bilbury felt (and Mr. Newman also) when he saw
the gentleman, whom he had last met as the tri-
coloured official of the Republic, passing through the
restaurant singing at the top of his voice and waving
his hand genially to the group as he went out upon
the boulevard.

But they remembered that in democracies the
office is distinguished from the man. Luckily for
democracies.

On a Battle, or "Journalism," or "Points of View" ~ ~

" The art of historical writing is rendered the less facile in expression from I know not what personal differences which the most honest will admit into their record of events, and the most observant will permit to colour the picture proceeding from their pens." (Extract from the Judicious Essay of a Gentleman in Holy Orders, author of *A History of Religious Differences.*)

I

From His Royal Highness the Commander-in-Chief to the Minister of War of his Brother the Emperor of Patagonia.

(Begins)

I HAVE the honour to report: Upon the morning of Sunday, the 31st, the enemy attacked the left of my position in great force, a little before dawn. I withdrew the XIth, XIIIth, and IInd Brigades, which were here somewhat advanced, covering their retirement with detachments from the First, the Thirty-seventh, and the Forty-second of the Line. The retirement was executed in good order and with small loss, the total extent of which I cannot yet determine, but of which by far the greater part consists of men but slightly wounded. Several pieces which had been irretrievably damaged were destroyed and abandoned. Upon reaching a position I had determined in my general plan before leaving the capital (see annexed sketch map A) the forces entrenched, defending a line which the enemy did not care to attack. I have reinforced the Brigade with two groups drawn from the Corps Artillery, and have despatched all aids, medicaments, etc., required.

A simultaneous attack delivered upon the centre of my position was repulsed, the enemy flying in the utmost disorder, and leaving behind them two pieces of artillery and a colour, which last I have sent under the care of Major the Duke of Tierra del Fuego to be deposited among the glorious trophies that adorn the Military Temple.

By noon the action showed no further development. In the early afternoon I determined to advance my right, largely reinforced from the centre, which was now completely secure from attack. The movement was wholly successful, and the result coincided exactly with my prearranged plans. The enemy abandoned all this upper portion of the right bank of the Tusco in the utmost confusion; his main body is therefore now in full retreat, and there is little doubt that over and above the decisive and probably final character of this success I shall be able to report in my next the capture of many prisoners, pieces, and stores. I congratulate His Majesty upon the conspicuous courage displayed in every rank, and recommend for distinguished service the 1847 names appended. His Majesty's Government may take it that this action virtually ends the war. (Ends.)

II

FROM FIELD-MARSHAL THE MOST ILLUSTRIOUS THE LORD DUKE OF RAPELLO TO THE MINISTER OF WAR OF THE REPUBLIC OF UTOPIA.

(Begins) Upon the morning of Sunday, the 31st, in accordance with the plan which I had drawn up before leaving the capital, I advanced my right a little before dawn against the left of the Imperial position, which was very strongly posted upon the edge of a precipitous cliff, one flank reposing upon an impassable gulf and the other on a deep and torrential river. The enemy resisted with the utmost stubbornness, but was eventually driven from his positions, though these were strongly entrenched after more than a week's work with the spade. He abandoned the whole of his artillery. A great number of prisoners have fallen into my hands, and the loss of the enemy in killed alone must amount to many thousands. Particulars will follow later, but I am justified in saying that the left wing of the enemy is totally destroyed. Meanwhile, General Mitza, most ably carrying out my instructions, con-

tained the enemy upon the centre without loss, save
for one pompom and a Maxim, which were shattered
by a chance shell early in the action. The 145th
also report the loss by burning of a waggon con-
taining their Colours, eighteen cans of tinned beef,
and the Missionaries' travelling library. Somewhat
later in the day the enemy attempted to retrieve a
hopeless position by advancing his right in great
force. I had been informed of the movement (which
was somewhat clumsily executed) in ample time, and
withdrew the petty outposts I had thrown out for
observation in his neighbourhood. There is little
doubt that the enemy will now attempt to withdraw
his main force along the line of the Tusco Valley,
but a glance at the map will show that this retreat
is closed to him by my occupation of the line X Y
(see annexed sketch map), and he is now virtually
contained.

I congratulate the Government of the Republic
upon the signal and decisive victory our troops have
driven home, and I may confidently assure them that
it is tantamount to the successful ending of the
present campaign. Appended is a list of officers
recommended for distinguished service, which I have
made as brief as possible, and which I particularly
beg after so glorious a day may not be curtailed by
political intrigues, of which I have already been
compelled to complain. (Ends.)

On Everything

III

Extract from a Leading Article in one of the most Reputable Newspapers of the Capital of Patagonia upon Monday the 1st.

"We have always maintained in these columns that His Imperial Majesty's Government was amply justified in undertaking the short, and now happily successful, campaign in which it was proposed to chastise the so-called 'Republic' of Utopia, whose chronic state of anarchy is a menace to the peace and prosperity of civilisation. It is a pleasure to be able to announce this morning what was already a foregone conclusion in the minds of all educated men. The enemy's forces—if we may dignify them by that name—have been overwhelmed at the first contact, and it is now only a question of whether they will be utterly disorganised during retreat or will prefer to capitulate while some semblance of discipline remains to them. We must, however, implore public opinion to preserve at this juncture the calm, sane courage which is among the best traditions of our race, and we reiterate the absolute necessity of abstaining from any wild cat policy of annexation. It should be enough for us that the 'Republic' of Utopia will now exist in name only, and has ceased for ever to be a menace to its neighbours. A specially gratifying feature in the news before us is the skill and mastery displayed by the Prince, whose advanced years (we blush to remember it) had been the cause of so much secret criticism of his command."

IV

EXTRACT FROM THE LEADING ARTICLE OF THE MOST POPULAR JOURNAL OF THE UTOPIAN REPUBLIC, SAME DATE.

"Citizens, awake! All ye that kneel, arise! Ares (the god of battles) has breathed upon the enemy, and he has been destroyed! The cowardly mercenaries who handle the gold of Patagonia have broken and fled before our troops upon the very first occasion when their reputed valour was put to the test. The glorious and aged Mitza has guaranteed that the next news will be that of their complete submission. It will then be for the Government to decide whether our victorious lads should complete a triumphant march upon the Patagonian capital or whether it may not be preferable to wring from that corrupt and moribund society such an indemnity as shall make them for ever impotent to disturb the frontiers of free men."

V

EXTRACT FROM THE NOTE OF THE MILITARY EXPERT OF THE AFORESAID WEIGHTY AND REPUTABLE JOURNAL OF THE CAPITAL OF PATAGONIA: A JOURNALIST.

"It is not easy to reconstruct from the fragmentary telegrams that have come through from the

front the tactical nature of the great and happily
decisive victory upon the Tusco which has just ended
the campaign. So far as one can judge, His Royal
Highness the Commander-in-Chief lay *en biais,* reposing his right upon the river itself and his left
upon the Cañon of the Encantado, his centre somewhat advanced 'in gabion,' his pivot points refused,
and his right in double concave. Upon a theory of
Ballistic and Shock, which all those who have read
His Royal Highness's daring and novel book of thirty
years ago, entitled 'Cavalry in the Field,' will remember, our Corps Artillery and reserve of horse
were doubtless some miles in the rear of the firing
line. The enemy, with an amazing ignorance of the
elements of military knowledge, appear to have
attacked the *left* of this position. It is an error to
which we should hardly give credence were not the
telegrams so clear and decisive on this point. The
reader will immediately grasp the obvious result of
such a piece of folly. His Royal Highness promptly
refused *en potence,* wheeled his left centre round upon
the Eleventh Brigade as a pivot, and supported this
masterly move by the sudden and unexpected appearance of no less than thirty-six guns, the con-
verging fire of which at once arrested the ill-fated
and mad scheme of the enemy. The rest is easily
told. Our centre retaining its position, in spite of
the burning zeal of the men to take part in the
general advance, the right, which had not yet come
into action, was thrown forward with a sudden,

sweeping movement, and behind its screen of Cavalry
debouched upon the open plateau which dominates
the left bank of the Tusco. After that all was over;
the next news we shall have will certainly be the
capitulation of our broken foe, unless, indeed, he
prefer to be destroyed piecemeal in a scattered
flight."

VI

EXTRACT FROM THE NOTE OF THE MILITARY EXPERT
OF THE POPULAR JOURNAL OF UTOPIA: FORMERLY
A SERGEANT IN THE COMMISSARIAT DEPARTMENT OF
THE ARMY.

"It is not easy to reconstruct from the fragmentary telegrams which have come through from
the front the tactical nature of the great and happily
decisive victory upon the Tusco. Some points are
obvious. In the first place, it was 'a soldiers' battle.'
Gallant old Mitz (to whom all honour is due) drew
up the line of battle, but the hard work was done
by Bill Smith and Tom Jones, and the rest in the
deadly trenches above the right bank. It seems
probable that all the heaviest work was done on our
right, and therefore against the enemy's left, unless,
indeed, the private telegram received by a contemporary be accurate, which would make out the
heaviest work to have been on our left against the
enemy's right. The present writer has an intimate
personal knowledge of the terrain, over every part

of which he rode during the manœuvres of five years ago. It is sandy in places, interspersed with damp, clayey bits ; much of it is undulating, and no small part of it rocky. Trees are scattered throughout the expanse of the now historic battlefield ; their trunks afford excellent cover. The River Tusco, as our readers will have observed, is the dominating feature of the quadrilateral, which it cuts *en échelon*. The Patagonians boasted that though our army was acknowledgedly superior to their own, their commercial position would enable them to weary us out in the field. Yes, I don't think ! "

VII

Extract from a Lecture delivered by a Professor of Military History one hundred years later, in the University of Lima.

" Among the minor factors of this complicated situation was the permanent quarrel between Patagonia and Utopia, and though it has been much neglected by historians, and is, indeed, but a detail upon the flank of the great struggle of the coalition, a few moments must be given to the abortive operations in the Tusco Valley. They appear to have been conducted without any grasp of the main rules of strategy, each party advancing in a more or less complete ignorance of the position of the other, their communications parallel, their rate of advance

deplorably slow, and neither possessing the information nor the initiative to strike at his opponent
during a three-weeks' march, at no point of which
was either army so much as fifty miles from the other.
These farcical three weeks ended in a sort of skir-
mish difficult to describe, and apparently confined
to the extreme left of the Patagonian forces. The
Utopians here effected some sort of confused advance,
which was soon checked. At the other end of the
line they retired before a partial movement of the
enemy, effected without any apparent object, and
certainly achieving no definite result. The total
losses in killed and wounded were less than seven per
cent of those engaged. The next day negotiations
were entered into between the two generals; their
weary discussion occupied a whole week, during
which hostilities were suspended. The upshot of
the whole thing was the retirement of the Patagonian Army under guarantees, and in consideration
of the acceptation of the old frontier by the Utopian
Government. Politically the campaign is beneath
notice, as both territories were absorbed six months
after in the recasting of the map after the Treaty of
Lima, and the policing of them handed over to the
now all-conquering Northern Power. Even as military history the operations deserve little more than
passing notice, save, perhaps, as an example of the
gross yet ever recurrent folly of placing numerically
large commands in the hands of aged men. Mitza,
upon the occasion of this fiasco, was over seventy-five

years of age and long in his dotage, while the Prince
of the Blood who had been chosen to lead (nominally, at least) the Patagonian Army was, apart from
his increasing years, a notorious drunkard, and what
is perhaps worse from a military point of view, daily
subject to long and complete lapses of memory."

A Descendant of William Shakespeare ⟳

IT was during the early months of 1909 that I first became acquainted with a descendant of William Shakespeare the great dramatist, who happened at that moment to be in London.

This gentleman (for he was of the male sex) was one of our American visitors, and was stopping at the Carlton Hotel. His name, as he assured me, Charlemagne K. Hopper. He resided, when he was at home, in the rapidly rising township of Bismarckville, Mo., where he added to a considerable private income the profits of a extensive corn business, dealing in wheat both white and red, and of both spring and autumn varieties, maize or Indian corn, oats, rye, buckwheat of every variety, seed corn, and bearded barley; indeed, no kind of cereal was unfamiliar to this merchant. His quick eye for the market and the geniality of his character had (he convinced me) made him friends in every circle. He has the entrée to the most exclusive coteries of Albany and Buffalo, and he had that season been received by the patrons of literature in Park Lane, Clarges Street, and Belgrave Square.

Mr. Hopper's descent from the Bard of Avon has been established but quite recently: these lines are perhaps the first to lay it before the public, and the discovery is an excellent example of the way in which two apparently insignificant pieces of evidence may, in combination, suggest an historical discovery of capital importance.

It is, of course, common knowledge that Lady Barnard of Abington was a lineal descendant of William Shakespeare. She died (without issue, as was until recently supposed) at the end of the seventeenth century. But two almost simultaneous finds made in the early part of the present year have tended to modify the old-established conviction that this lady was the last descendant of the poet.

The first of these finds was made by Mr. Vesey, of the British Museum, well known for his monograph on *The Family of Barnard of Abington*. It consisted in a small diary or notebook belonging to the Lady Barnard in question, in which, among other entries, was the record of the payment of twenty guineas made to a "Mrs. M." just before Christmas of the year 1678. Mr. Vesey published this document in pamphlet form at the beginning of March, 1908.

In the April number of *Cambridgeshire Notes and Queries* Major Pepper, of Bellevue Villa, Teversham (not far from the Gog Magog Hills), published, as a matter of curiosity, a letter which he had purchased in a sale of MSS., but only so published on the chance that it might have an interest for those who follow the history of the county. It was a

A Descendant of William Shakespeare

letter from one Joan Mandrell, the governess of Anne Hall, praying her correspondent to send "twenty guineas for the payment of rent." The interest of this document to the students of local history lay in the fact that this Anne Hall was the ancestress of the Pooke family. Joan Mandrell's letter was addressed upon the back of the sheet, though the name of the addressee was no longer decipherable, but the letters ". . . . bington Hall" were, and are, clearly legible, as also the date. The letter further contains a minute description of Anne Hall's return to London from a foreign school and of the writer's devotion to the addressee, whom she treats throughout as mother of the young woman committed to her care. This Anne Hall later married Henry Pooke, whose son Charles made his fortune in politics under Walpole's administration, founding the family and estate of Understoke, which is so familiar to every Cambridgeshire man.

More than one student noted the coincidence between these two publications appearing but a fortnight apart; and at the end of May a paper was already prepared to be read to the Genealogical Society showing that the lineage of the poet had been continued in the Pookes.

So far the matter was of merely antiquarian interest, for Charles Pooke's great grandson, General Sir Arthur Pooke, had died in 1823 at Understoke without issue. It was, however, of some importance to all those who care for the literary history of their country to know that the blood of the poet could be traced so far.

Just before the paper was read a further discovery came in to add a much greater and more living interest to the matter.

Mr. Cohen, a charming and cultivated genealogist, whose business is mainly with America and the Colonies, had been for some months actively engaged for Mr. Hopper in tracing the arms of his, Mr. Hopper's, maternal grandfather—a Mr. Pooke. When Mr. Cohen became acquainted with the facts mentioned above he cabled to Mr. Hopper, who sent by return of post copies of certain family documents which clearly proved that this Mr. Pooke was identical with a younger brother of Sir Arthur. This younger brother was an erratic and headstrong lad who had enlisted in early youth under Cornwallis, and had been killed, as it was believed, at York-town. He was as a fact wounded and made prisoner; he was not killed. He was released at the Peace of 1783, preferred remaining in the New World to facing his creditors in the Old, married the daughter of Peter Kymers, of Orange, N.J., and soon afterwards went West. In 1840 his only daughter Cassiopea, who was then keeping a small store in Cincinnati, married the Rev. Mr. Aesop Hopper, a local minister of the Hicksite persuasion. Charlemagne K. Hopper is the only issue of that marriage.

The genealogy stands thus :

A Descendant of William Shakespeare

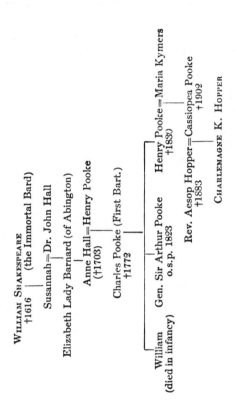

WILLIAM SHAKESPEARE †1616 ─── (the Immortal Bard)

Susannah=Dr. John Hall

Elizabeth Lady Barnard (of Abington)

Anne Hall=Henry Pooke (†1703)

Charles Pooke (First Bart.) †1772

William (died in infancy)

Gen. Sir Arthur Pooke o.s.p. 1823

Henry Pooke=Maria Kymers †1830

Rev. Aesop Hopper=Cassiopea Pooke †1883 †1902

CHARLEMAGNE K. HOPPER

On Everything

This family tree is now so well established that a full publication of the lineage, with a commentary upon the whole romantic story, is about to appear in one of the reviews from the pen of "Thersites," a pseudonym which, as many of our readers are aware, barely hides the identity of one of our best-known experts upon Foreign Affairs.[1]

Mr. Hopper did not remain in London beyond the close of the season. He had proposed to leave for Biskra a week or so after I made his acquaintance, but the change in the weather decided him to go no farther south than Palermo, whence he will return by Naples, Rome, Assisi, Genoa, and Boulogne, visiting on the way the quaint old city of Strasbourg. He will reach England again some time in the month of April, 1910, and on his return he proposes to devote some part of his considerable fortune to the erection of a suitable monument at Stratford-on-Avon in memory of his great ancestor. This generous gift will be accompanied by certain conditions, but there is little doubt that the town will accept the same, and that a fine fountain surrounded with symbolical figures of Justice, Prudence, and Mercy, and adorned with medallions of Queens Elizabeth and Victoria, George Washington and President Roosevelt, will soon adorn the quiet little Warwickshire town.

Mr. Hopper also proposes to found a Shakespeare

[1] Mr. H. Abrahims, of Eastcheap and The Firs, Guild-ford, Surrey.

A Descendant of William Shakespeare

Scholarship at Sidney-Sussex College in Cambridge, and another at Wadham College in Oxford, each of the value of £300 a year, on the model of the Rhodes Scholarships, such scholarships to be granted not merely for book work but for business capacity and physical development. He has also planned a Chair for the propagation of Shakespearean knowledge in Glasgow, and he will endow a Reader in Shakespeare to the University of Aberdeen.

Mr. Hopper is himself no mean *littérateur*, though a characteristic modesty has hitherto restrained him from publishing his verse, whether rhyme, blank, or in sonnet form. It is possible that now he is acquainted with his great descent his reluctance may be overcome and he may think better of this decision. I may add that Mr. Hopper places no credence in the Baconian theory, and hopes by diligent search among his family papers to prove the authenticity of at least the five major tragedies and *A Midsummer Night's Dream*.

Mr. Hopper is a total abstainer; he neither smokes nor chews; his religious views, always broad and tolerant, incline him strongly towards the New Theology, and, in common with many other men of exceptional intelligence, he has been profoundly affected by the popular translation of Dr. Haeckel's *Riddle of the Universe*.

Though delighting in social intercourse, Mr. Hopper has the true gentleman's instinct against being lionised, and in particular stands in dread of the Duchess of Dundee. He has therefore begged me to insist as little as possible on his identity in anything I thought it my duty to record in print upon so interesting a matter, and I have so far acceded to his request as to have refrained from publishing these lines until he had left our shores; but I make little doubt that on his return in the spring this missing link between the two branches of the Anglo-Saxon kin cannot but receive the public recognition he deserves.

On the Approach to Western England ∽

HOW difficult it is to say what one really feels about the landscapes and the countrysides and the subtle souls of Europe! I think that all men who are of European blood feel those countrysides and the soul of them very strongly; but I think that they feel as I feel now, as I write, a difficulty of expression. There is something in it like the difficulty of approaching a personality. One may admire, or reverence, or even love, but the personality is different from one's own; it has a chastity of its own that must be respected, it has its boundaries and its honour, and one always fears that one will transgress such boundaries if one so much as speaks of the new thing one has come upon and desired to describe.

With distant travel it is not so. One comes far over seas to a quite strange land and one treats it brutally. One's appreciation is a sort of conquest; and you will note that those who speak of the Colonies, or of America, or of Africa, or of Asia speak of them with a hard intolerance as of something quite alien, or with a conventional set of phrases, as of something not worth the real expression of emotion. Now it is not so with our ancient provinces of Europe.

167

On Everything

A man coming out of the Cis-Alpine Gaul into
old Italy across the Apennines feels something; indeed he feels it! What it is he feels very few men
have written down; none has said it fully. You
get out of one thing into something other when you
climb up out of the Valley of the Parma and cross
the High Apennines and look southward into the
happy Garfagnana, and hear the noise of the little
Serchio beginning in its meads. In the same way
no one has described (to my knowledge at least)
that shock of desolation and yet of mystery which
comes upon a man when he crosses the River
Couesnon and passes from Normandy into Brittany.
Normandy is rich, Brittany is poor. Normandy
loves ritual, Brittany religion. Normandy can make
things, Brittany prayers. Normandy lives by Brittany in the matter of the soul, Brittany not by
Normandy in the matter of the body. What Nor-
man ever gave a Breton anything? You cross that
river and everything changes. The men and women
have dreamier eyes, the little children play more
wonderfully, everybody is poor.

Or, again, the passage from the hard industry of
the Lancashire Plain suddenly on to the moors,
where the farming men and women are so quiet and
silent and self-respectful and seem so careful rather
to preserve what they own than to add to it. Or,
again, the startling passage over Carter Fell from
the Englishmen of Rede-Dale to the Scotchmen of
Jedburgh; or the sharp passage from the violent,

active, sceptical, cruel, courageous, well-fed, ironical Burgundians into the gentle Germans of the Vosges : here is a boundary which is not marked in any political way, and yet how marked it is !

Now in England we have many such approaches and surprises. I will not speak of that good change which comes upon a man as he travels south from Victoria Station and hears, almost at the same time that he first smells earth, the South Country tongue; nor will I speak of that other change which perhaps some of my readers know very well, the change from the active and grasping Cockney into the quiet tenacity of East Anglia. It is not my province— but if I am not wrong one strikes it within half an hour in the fast expresses—these people push with quants, they sail in wherries, they inhabit flat tidal banks, they are at peace. Nor will I here speak of the Marches and how, between a village and a village, one changes from the common English parish with the Squire's house and the church and the cottages and all, into the hard slate roofs and the inner flame of Wales. Rather I would speak of something the boundary of which has never yet been laid down, but which people call (I think) "The West Country."

.   .   .   .   .   .

One never knows, when one is tackling a thing like this, where one should first begin to tackle it, or by what end one should take it. Every man

according to his own study, every man according to
his own bent or accident of experience, takes it by
his own handle, and the one man speaks of the
language, the other of the hills, another of the
architecture, another of the names. For my part
I would desire to speak of all.

When one gets over a certain boundary one is in
a peculiar district of this world, a special countryside
of Europe, a happy land with a conviction and
a tradition of its own which may not have a name,
but which is in general the West Country, and
which by its hills and by its men and women con-
vinces any true traveller at once of its personality.
More than one man after a dreary wandering southwards through the Midlands has walked by night
up one of its fresh streets to an inn and cried:
" What! Have I come upon Paradise?" And this
feeling comes also when one has climbed up the
Cotswold through the little places of stone and
suddenly sees the valley floor of the Severn so full
of orchards, or has come over the flat deserts of the
Upper Thames and had revealed to him the Golden
Valley; or, after plodding through Wiltshire, has
smelt an air which told him that not far off were the
heavy tides of that haunted sea which runs between
the Welsh hills and the peninsula of Cornwall and
Devon. Men are lost in these seas and are saved in
them perpetually as by miracles: I can appeal, in
this print, to how many? They have been saved
by the miracle of that water. Here Arthur was

On the Approach to Western England

cast up by the waves : on to that flat salt, in its
calm, full of mists, looked out those who gave us
our legend of his Court.

The boundary into this particular land is not only
fetched by men on foot ; in no matter what kind of
travel one pursues, one recognises that boundary in
a flash as one traverses it. It is not only the orchards,
nor the abrupt and pointed hills, nor those domestic
towns, happy with memories, nor those clear waters,
nor those meadows, bounded by careful walls of
stone, but something much more which tells one that
one has got into the enchanted land. That spirit in
it which made the stuff of our early history, which
gave us the landing of Joseph of Arimathea and the
glorious bush of Glastonbury and the cycle of the
Round Table and those good verses with regard to
passion unrestrained :

> . . . . well you wot that of such life
> There comes but sore battaille and strife
> And blood of men and hard Travail . . . .

And the prophecies of Merlin, and the story of
Tristan and Iseult and all the vision of immortality
and of resurrection inhabits it still.

I never can believe (I speak for myself alone) that
man can be dissociated from his earth any more than
I can believe that the soul can be dissociated from
the body. When men say to me that there is
no soul, they can go on saying. But when men say
that the soul can neglect the body then there is

171

matter for argument; and when the argument is finished one finds it is not so. Now thus it is with the earth that breeds us and into which if we are content to die at home (and since we must die some-where, better die there) we should at last return. The landscapes of Europe make European men, and it is not for nothing that the climate and the shapes of the hills and the nature of the building stuff change just where man changes.

There is enchantment upon every high place of England, but the enchantment of the Devonshire Moors and of the Tors to the North and upwards from them is different from the enchantment of the Downs. There is a great delight in the proper fire-places of the English people, but who, thoroughly alive, could mistake a fireplace in the West Riding for a fireplace on the Western Rother or either of these for a fireplace a little before Sherborne in the tumbles and the hollows where Dorset and Somerset meet? There is a richness of the speech and a con-tentment of the tongue which any man from the new countries might think common to all English agricul-tural men: yet there was a man from Sussex who, hearing the Sussex tongue in the Choughs at Yeovil, felt himself indeed come home. Our provinces differ very much.

I have sometimes wondered whether in the pro-cess of time these little intimate differences of ours will survive. I wish they would! I wish they would, by the Lord! The Greeks were a little people, yet their provinces have survived, and the contempt that Aspasia felt for the Peloponnesus is (or should be) yet recorded. The hill tribes behind the Phœnician coast were a little people, but the fame of their religion, of their civil wars, has survived that of the merchants of Tyre. Rome, Veii, and the others were little places like Arundel and Pulborough, quite close together; but they were talked of, and men know much of them to-day.

I could wish the differences of this island were so known and that people coming from a long way off would be humble and learn those differences. Surely a nation grows great in this way, by many provinces reacting one upon the other, recognised by the general will, sometimes in conflict with it. At any rate the West Country is a province of Europe; no one can get into it without touching his youth again and putting his fingers to earth, and getting sustenance from it, as a man does when he turns at the turning point of a race and touches earth with his fingers and is strong again to spring forward.

The Weald   ∽   ∽   ∽   ∽   ∽

AMONG the changes that have come upon England with the practice and facility for rapid
travel many would put first the conquest (some
would call it the spoiling) of little-known and
isolated stretches of English landscape; and men
still point out with a sort of jealous pride those districts, such as the upper Cotswolds, which modern
travel has not disturbed. It seems to me that there is
another feature attaching to the facility for travel, and
that is this, that men can now tell other men what
their countrysides are like ; men can now compare
one part of England with another in a way that once
they could not do, and this facility in communication
which so many deplore has so much good about it
at least, in that it permits right judgments. There
have been men in the past who have travelled
widely for the mere pleasure of seeing many parts
of their own country—Cobbett was one—but they
were rare. As the towns grew, commercial travelling led men only to the towns, but now the thing is
settling down. Men travel everywhere, all kinds of
men, and no part of England remains of which a
man can say that he loves it without knowing why
he loves it, or that its character is indefinable. So
it is with the Weald.

The Weald

All that roll of land which lies held between and above the chalk of South-Eastern England, the clay and the sand, and the uncontinuous short trees, the muddy little rivers, the scattered homesteads, the absence of levels, and almost the absence of true hills, the distant prospects northwards and southwards of quite another land, the blue lines and naked heights a day's journey away against the sky —all that is the Weald. And it runs from the place where the two lines of chalk meet in Hampshire beyond Selborne, and beyond Petersfield, right away to the sea which it sweeps upon in a grand curve, between Pevensey (which was once the chief port of the Weald) and the heights round Hastings : for though these heights are in a manner part of the Weald, yet between them and the chalk again by Folkestone no true Wealden country lies.

Unless a man understands the Weald he cannot easily write about the beginnings of England, and yet historians have not understood it. Only the men mixed into it and married with it or born upon it have understood it, and these, I say, until lately were not permitted by constant travel that judgment by analogy and by contrast which teaches us the true meaning of things that we had hitherto only instinctively known. Now a Wealden man can say certain things about his countryside which are of real value to history and perhaps to politics as well ; at any rate, to politics in that larger sense of patriotism intelligently appreciating the future of one's own

lanu. Thus the Wealden man, now that he knows
so much else in England, can tell the historian that
the Weald was never the impenetrable forest which
historians would make of it. It lay in a barrier
between the ports of the Channel and the Thames
Valley. But the barrier was not uninhabited; it was
not impassable. Its scattered brushwood was patchy,
its soil never permanently marshy nor ever for long
distances difficult for a mounted man or a man on
foot. The Weald from the very beginning had
homesteads in it, but it had not agglomerations
of houses, nor had it parishes save in very few places.
If you look at the map now you can see how the old
parishes stretch northward and southward in long
strips from the chalk and loam country up towards
the forest ridge which is the centre of the Weald.
Those long strips were the hunting rights of the
village folk and their lords. Of some parishes carved
out of the central Weald we can accurately tell the
origin. We know that they were colonised as it
were, cleared, and had their church built for them in
the great spurt of civilisation which marked the
twelfth and thirteenth centuries. Men would understand the early history of the Weald better, and
with it the early military history of South-Eastern
England, if they would take one of the old forest
paths—as that from Rusper, for instance, which
works its way down, now as a metalled road, now as
a green lane, now as a mere footpath with right
of way, past the two old " broad " fords on the upper

The Weald

Arun and the marshy land east of Pulborough until
it gets to Roundabout, and so to Storrington. All
the history of communications in the Weald is ex-
emplified in such a journey—and it is a journey which,
though it is little more than twenty miles in length,
takes quite a day. You have the modern high road,
the green lane of the immediate past, and in places
a mere track of remote antiquity. You see just how
difficult it is to traverse the clay, how the occasional
knobs of sand relieve your going; you can notice the
character of the woodland where it is still untouched,
and if you are wise you will notice one thing above
all, and that is the character of the water. Now it
is this which explains the Weald. Many bad bits
of clay in Europe have formed highways for armies
—for instance, all that rotten land in the great bend
of the Loire which the Romans called the *Solitarium*,
and which the French called the *Sologne*. But the
Weald differs from most others in this, that good and
plentiful water is hard to find. It is not the muddi-
ness of the streams that is the chief defence of the
place against human travel and habitation; it is the
way in which, when rain has fallen and when water
is plentiful, going is difficult, and the way in which,
when a few days of dry weather come, the going
becomes easy, but the water in the little streams
disappears. There is evidence that the Romans, when
they built their great military road—perhaps their
only purely military road in Britain—across the
Weald skipped one intervening station which should,

upon the analogy of others, have been present upon it in the heart of the Weald, and pressed the march in this place to nearly double its usual length. The French armies do precisely the same thing in the bad lands of the Plain of Chalons to-day. Wherever there is ancient habitation in the Weald, or rather upon the fringes of the Weald, there is good, plentiful, and perennial water; elsewhere the Weald is still what it has been throughout history—a great rolling place, not deserted, not lonely, and yet not humanised. It is exactly the place for a seclusion from men, for you can see some men, but not too many of them; and I have always thought that King wise, who, when his enemies desired to kill him, wandered in the Andredsweald. The historians say that he took refuge in the impassable thickets of the forest. This is bosh. No man can sleep out in this climate for a season round, nor can any man live without cooked meat, nor do I see an Anglo-Saxon king living without wine and a good deal of pomp into the bargain. As to the wine, men might argue, but as to the pomp, they cannot. I will tell you what this King did without any doubt. He went from steading to steading and was royally entertained, and if you ask why it was a refuge for him the answer is that it was a refuge against the pursuit of many men.

The Weald is a refuge against the pursuit of many men. It was so then: it is so now.

And this leads me to my conclusion. The Weald

The Weald

will never be conquered. It will always be the
Weald. To be conquered is to suffer the will of
another : the Weald will suffer no will but its own.
The men of the Weald drive out men odious to them
in manner sometimes subtle, sometimes brutal,
always in the long run successful. Economics break
against the Weald as water breaks against stone. It
is not a long walk from London. Your Londoner in
summer comes and builds in it. So foreign birds
their nests. But unlike the foreign birds, he does
not return with each returning spring. For the
Weald will welcome the bird for the pleasure the
bird gives it, and drive it out when the pleasure is
done. Now it welcomes the Londoner for his money,
and this feature in the Londoner is not recurrent
with the seasons.

Here is some Latin which I am assured is gram-
matical and correctly spelled as well :

Stat et stabit : manet et manebit, spectator orbis.

She stands and still shall stand ; she remains and
shall remain : a watcher of the generations.

On London and the Houses in it ∽ ∽

THE aspect of London, as the man who knows it grows older, begins to take on characters of permanence and characters of change, both of which are comparable to those of a human life. It is perceived that certain qualities in the great soul of the place are permanent, and that the memories of many common details merge after the passage of years into a general picture which is steadfast and gives unity to the whole.

This is especially true of the London skies, and more true, I think, of the London skies in autumn than at any other season of the year. Men go home from the City or from the Courts westward at an hour which is that of sunset, when the river catches more light than at any other time : the mixture of mist and smoke and of those shapes in our clouds, beyond the reek of the town, which are determined by the south-west wind blowing up the line of the valley, make together an impression which is the most lasting of the landscapes in which we live. These it was which inspired Turner when he drew them from the deserted room in the tower of Battersea Church, or from that corner house over the River, whence he could watch evening after evening the

On London and the Houses in it

heavy but transparent colours which enter into the things he painted. Many foreigners, caught by the glamour of that artist, have missed the source whence his mellow and declining sunlight was inspired; its source was in these evening and autumn skies of London. There is a permanence also in the type of home which London built for more than two centuries, and which was laid down after the Great Fire, and there is a permanence in the older stonework. It is difficult or impossible to define what there is in common between the brown stock brick of London, which is the stuff of all its background whether of large houses or mean, and the black and white weathering of Portland stone. Perhaps the unity which seems to bind them is wholly in the mind, and depends merely upon association, but it is very strong upon anyone who has grown up from childhood into middle age surrounded by the vision of this town; and it would seem as though London was only London because of those rough surfaces of soft stonework, streaked with white wedges, scaling off the grime of St. Martin's, or St. Clement Dane's, or the fine front of the Admiralty, and standing out clear against the general brown mass of the streets. The quite new things have no character at all. One wonders what cosmopolitan need can have produced them. London never produced them, with their stone that so often is plaster, and their alien suggestion of whatever is least national in Paris or New York. London never produced them.

On Everything

The noise of the streets in spite of every change remains the same, it is the same comforting and distant roar, like the roar of large waters among hills, which every visitor has noticed, with its sharp contrast to the rattle and cries of other great capitals. Why it should be so no one, I think, has discovered, though many have described it, but it remains an unmistakable thing, and if a London man, who had travelled and was far away, should be set down by a spirit in London, not knowing where he was, when he heard through a window high above the street this distant and continuous roar, he would know that he had come home. It should surely in theory have disappeared, this chief physical characteristic of the great place, yet neither the new electricity and the hissing of the wires, nor the new paving, nor even the new petrol seem to change it. It is still a confused and powerful and subdued voice, like a multitude undecided. The silence also does not change. The way in which in countless spots you pass through an unobserved low passage, or through an inconspicuous narrow turning, and find yourself in a deserted place, from which the whole life of London seems blanketed out, has been to every traveller and to every native part of the charm and surprise of London. Dickens knew it very well, and makes of it again and again a dramatic something in his work which stamps it everywhere with the soul of London. In every decade men growing older deplore the disappearance of this or that sanc-

tuary of isolation and silence, but in the aggregate
they never disappear ; something in the very character of the people reproduces them continually,
and if any man will borrow the leisure—even a
man who knows his London well—to peer about
and to explore for one Saturday afternoon in one
square mile of older London, how many such unknown corners will he not find ! The populace also
upon whom all this is founded remain the same.

What changes in London are the things that also
change in the life of a man, and nothing more than
the relationship of particular spots and particular
houses to our own lives. There is perhaps no city
in the world where, under the permanence of the
general type, there is so perpetual a flow and disturbance of association. It has even become normal
to the life of the citizens, and the conception of a
fixed home has left them. Here and there—but
more and more rarely with every year—you may
point out a great house which some wealthy family
has chosen to inhabit for some few generations ; but
fixity of tenure, tradition, family tradition at least,
and sacred hereditary things, either these were never
proper to London or they have gone; it is this which
overspreads a continued knowledge of London with
an increasing loneliness and with memories that find
no satisfaction or expression, but re-enter the heart
of a man and do a hurt to him there.

There are so many strange doors that should be
familiar doors. Turning sometimes into some street

On Everything

where one has turned for years to find at a very well-
known number windows of a certain aspect and little
details in the drab exterior of the house, every one
of which was as familiar as a smile, one is (by the
mere association of years and of a gesture repeated
a thousand times) in the act of coming to the steps
and of seeking an entry. The whole place is as
much one's friend and as much indicative of one's
friend as would be his clothes or his voice or any
other external thing. He is not there, and the
house is worse than empty. London grows full of
such houses as a man grows older. Most of us have
other losses sharper still, which men of other cities
know less well, for most of us pass and repass the
house where we were born, or where as children we
gathered all the strongest impressions of life. It is
impossible to believe that other souls are inheriting
the effect of those familiar rooms. It is worse than
a death; it is a kind of treason.

I know a house in Wimpole Street of which every
part is as familiar quite as the torn leaves of the old
books of childhood, but I have passed it and re-
passed it for how many years, forbidden an entrance,
and finding that ancient and fixed friend in league,
so to speak, with strangers. Or, in another manner,
which of us does not know a house like any other
house, amid the thousand unmarked houses in the
better streets of the town, but to us quite individual
because there met within it once so many who were
for us the history of our time? It was in that room

(where are the three windows) that she received her
guests, retaining on into the last generations of a
worse and degraded time the traditions of a better
society. Here came men who could discuss and
reveal things that are now distorted legends, and
whose revelations were real because they came as
witnesses: soldiers of the Crimea, of India, of
Italy, and of Algiers, or men who remembered
great actions within the State: actions that were
significant through conviction, before we became
what we are. Here was breeding; here were the
just limits of tone and emphasis and change, and
here was that type of intercourse which was surely
as great and as good a thing as Europe or England
has known. Who sees that room to-day? What
taste has replaced her taste? What choice of stuff
or colour mars the decoration on the walls? What
trash or alien thing takes the place of that careful
elaborate womanly work in which her travels
throughout the world were recorded, and in which
the excellent modesty of an art sufficient for her
purpose reproduced in line and in colour the ironic
nobility of her mind and the wide expanse of her
learning? We do not know and we cannot know.
The house is neither ours nor hers. To whomever
it has passed it has turned traitor to us who knew.

It is better, I think, for those who have such memories when the material things that enshrine them
wholly disappear, for then there is no jar, no agony
of contrast between that society which once was and

this which now is, with its quality of wealth and of the uses to which wealth is put to-day. If we must suffer the intolerable and clumsy presence of accidental power—power got suddenly, got anyhow, got by chance, untrained and unworthy—at least may we suffer such things in their own surroundings, in huge conservatories, with loud music, with an impression of partial drunkenness all around, and a certainty all around of intellectual incompetence and of sprawling bodies and souls. It is better to suffer these new things in such surroundings as may easily let one believe that one is not in London at all, but on the Riviera; and let the heat be excessive, and let there be a complete ignorance of all wine except champagne, and let it be a place where champagne is supposed to be one wine. Then the frame will suit the picture, and there will at least be no desecration of material things by human beings unworthy of the bricks and mortar. I say it is much better when the old houses disappear, at least the old houses in which we knew and loved the better people of a better time :—and yet the youth or childhood in which so many of us saw the last of it is not thirty years, is barely twenty years dead !

On Old Towns ∽ ∽ ∽ ∽ ∽

EVERY man who has a civilised backing behind him, every man, that is, born to a citizenship which has history to nourish it, knows, loves, desires to inhabit, and returns to, the Old Towns; but the more one thinks of it the more difficult one finds it to determine in what this appetite consists.

The love of a village, of a manor, is one thing. You may stand in some place where you were born or brought up, especially if it be some place in which you passed those years in which the soul is formed to the body, between, say, seven years of age and seventeen, and you may look at the landscape of it from its height, but you will not be able to determine how much in your strong affection is of man and how much of God. True, nearly everything in a good European landscape has been moulded, touched, coloured, and in a sense made by Christian men. It is like a sort of tapestry which man has worked upon the stuff that God gave him; but, still, any such landscape from the height of one of our villages has surely more in it of God than of man. For one thing there is the sky; and then it must be admitted that the lines of the hills were there before man touched them, and though the definite outline

187

of the woods, the careful thinning of them which allows great trees to grow, the noble choice and contrast of foliage, the sharp edge of cultivated against forest land, the careful planting of the tallest kinds of things, pine trees and elms, are all man's work; and though the sights of water in between are usually man's work also, yet in the air that clothes the scene and in all its major lines, man did not make it at all: he has but used it and improved it under the inspiration of That which made the whole.

But with the Old Towns it is not so. They please us in proportion to their apparent intensity of effort; the more man has worked the more can we embed ourselves within them. The more different is every stone from another, and the more that difference is due to the curious spirit of man the more are we pleased. We stand in little lanes where every single thing about us, except the strip of sky overhead, is man's work, and the strip of sky overhead becomes what all skies are in all pictures—something subordinate to man, an ornament.

One could make a list of the Old Towns and go on for ever: the sea-light over the red-brick of King's Lynn from the east, and the other sea-light from the south over that other King's town, Lyme Regis; the curious bunch of Rye; the hill of Poitiers all massed up with history, and in whose uneven alleys all the armies go by, from the armies of the Gauls to the army that makes a noise about them to-day. the hill of Lincoln, where one looks up

from the Roman Gate to the towers completing the
steep hill; the two hills of Cassel and of Montreuil,
similarly packed with all that men are, have been,
and remain; the quadrated towns, some surely
Roman, some certainly so; Chichester, Winchester,
Horsham, Oxford, Chester, and a hundred others—
England is most fruitful in these; the towns that
draw their life from rivers and have high steep walls
of stone or brick going right down into the waters,
Albi, Newcastle as it once was; in its own small way
Arundel as it still is; the towns of the great flats,
where men for some reason can best give rein to
their fancy, Delft, Antwerp (that part of it which
counts), Bruges, Louvain; Ypres also where the cook-
ing is so vile.

One might continue for ever this futile list of
towns—this is in common to them all, that where-
ever men come across them in travel they have a
sense of home and the soul reposes.

Nowhere have I found this more than in the
curious and to some the disappointing town of Arles.
Arles has about it, more than any other town I know,
the sentiment of protracted human experience. They
dig and find stone tools and weapons. They dig
again and find marks of log huts, bronze pins, and
the arms of the Gauls. And then, apparent to the
eye and still living as it were, and still breathing, as
it were, the upper air which is also ours, not buried
away like dead things, but surviving, is Greece, is
Rome, is the Dark Ages, is the Middle Ages, is the

Renaissance, is the religious quarrel, is the Eighteenth
Century, is the Revolution, is to-day. I have sometimes thought that if a man should go to Arles with
the desire deliberately to subject himself at once to
the illusion and to the reality of the past, here he
could do so. He could look curiously for a day at
the map and see how the Rhone had swept the place
for thousands upon thousands of years, making it a
sort of corner at the head of its great estuary, and
later of its delta; then he might spend the day
wondering at the flints and the way they were
chipped, and getting into the minds of the men that
made them. Then he should spend a day with
bronze, and then a day with the Gaulish iron. After
that, for as many weeks as he chose, let him study
the stones which Greece and which Rome have still
left in the public places of the city ; the half of the
frontal of the great temple built into his hotel ;
the amphitheatre upon which he suddenly comes as
he wanders up a narrow modern street; the Arenæ.
The Dark Ages, which have left so little in Europe,
have here left massive towers in which the echoes
of the fighting linger, and huge rough stones which
the Dark Ages did not quarry but which they moved
from the palaces of the Romans to their own fortresses, and which by their very presence so removed
bring back to one the long generations in which
Europe slept healthily and survived.

St. Trophime is all the Middle Ages. You may
walk quietly round its cloister and see those ten

generations of men, from the hugeness of the Crusades to the last delicacies of the fifteenth century. The capitals of the columns go in order, the very earliest touch on that archaic grotesque which underlies every civilisation, the latest in their exact realism and their refinement, prove the decline of a whole period of the soul. Lest Arles should take up too much of this short space, I would remind the reader only of this ironical and striking thing: that on its gates as you go out of the city northward, you may see sculptured in marble what the Revolution—but a century ago—took to be a primal truth common to all mankind. It concerns the sanctity of property. Consider that doctrine to-day!

But not Arles, though it is so particular an example, not Delft, not the old English seaports which so perfectly enshrine our past, not Coutances which everyone should know, alone explain what the Old Towns are, but rather a knowledge of them all together explains it.

The Old Towns are ourselves; they are mankind. In their contortion, in their ruined regularity, in their familiar oddities, and in their awful corners of darkness, in their piled experience of the soul which has soaked right into their stone and their brick and their lime, they are the caskets of man. Note how the trees that grow by licence from the crevices of their battlements are a sort of sacramental saving things, exceptional to the fixed lines about them, and note how the grass which grows between the setts of their paving stones comes up ashamedly and yet universally, as good memories do in the oldness of the human mind, and as purity does through the complexity of living.

Which reminds me: Once there was a band of men, foolish men, Bohemian men, indebted men, who went down to paint in a silly manner, and chose a town of this sort which looked to them very old and wonderful; and there they squatted for a late summer month and talked the detestable jargon of their trade. They talked of tones and of values and of the Square Touch, and Heaven knows what nonsense, the meanwhile daubing daub upon daub on to the canvas; praising Velasquez (which after all was right) and ridiculing the Royal Academy. They ridiculed the Royal Academy.

Well, now, these men were pleased to see in autumn grass growing between the setts of the street, especially in one steep street where they lived. It rejoiced their hearts; they said within themselves, "This is indeed an Old Town!" But the Town Council of that town had said among themselves, "What if it become publicly known that grass grows in our streets? We shall be thought backward; the rich will not come to visit us. We shall not make so much money, and our brothers-in-law and others indebted to us will also grow impoverished. Come! Let us pull up this grass."

On Old Towns

So they paid a poor man, who would otherwise have starved, the amount of his food on the condition that he should painfully pull up all the grass, which he did.

Then the artists, seeing him at work, paid him more not to pull it up. Then the Town Council, finding out this, dismissed him from their employ, and put upon the job a distant man from some outlandish county, and had him watched, and he pulled up all the grass, every blade of it, by night, but thoroughly. The next morning the artists saw what had been done, and they went out by train to another town, and bought grass seed and also a little garden soil, and the next night they scattered the soil carefully between the stones and sowed the grass seed; and the comedy is not yet ended.

There is a moral to this, but I will not write it down, for in the first place it may not be a good moral, and in the second place I have forgotten what it was.

A Crossing of the Hills ❧ ❧ ❧

WHEN it was nearly noon my companion said to me:

"By what sign or track do you propose to cross the mountains?" For the mountains here seem higher than any of highest clouds: the valley beneath them is broad and full of fields: beyond, a long day off, stands in a huge white wall the Sierra del Cadi. Yet we must cross these hills if ever we were to see the secluded and little-known Andorrans. For the Andorrans live in a sort of cup fenced in on every side by the Pyrenees; it was on this account that my companion asked me how I would cross over to their land and by what sign I should find my way.

When I had thought a little I answered:

"By none. I propose to go right up at them, and over unless I find some accident by which I am debarred."

"Why, then," said he, "let us strike up at once, walking steeply until we come into a new country."

This advice was good, and so, though we had no longer any path, and though a mist fell upon us, we began walking upwards, and it was like going up a moor in the West Riding, except that it went on

A Crossing of the Hills

and on and on, hour after hour, and was so steep
that now and then one had to use one's hands.

The mist was all round us; it made a complete
silence, and it drifted in the oddest way, making
wisps of vapour quite close to our faces. Nor had
we any guide except the steepness of the hill. For
it is a rule when you are caught in a storm or mist
upon the hills, if you are going up, to go the steep-
est way, and though in such a fog this often took us
over a knoll which we had to descend again, yet on
the whole it proved a very good rule. It was perhaps the middle of the afternoon, we had been
climbing some five hours, we had ascended some six
thousand or seven thousand feet, when to our vast
astonishment we stumbled upon a sort of road.

It must here be explained why we were astonished. The way we had come led nowhere; there
were no houses and no men. The Andorrans whom
we were about to visit have no communication
northward with the outer world except a thin wire
leading over the hills, by which those who wish to
telephone to them can do so; and of all places in
Europe, Andorra is the place out of which men
least desire to get and to which men least desire
to go. It is like that place beyond Death of which
people say that it gives ccmplete satisfaction and
from which certainly no one makes any effort to
escape, and yet to which no one is very anxious to
go. When, therefore, we came to this road, beginning suddenly half way up a bare mountain and

appearing unexplained through the mist, we were astonished.

It was embanked and entrenched and levelled as would be any great French military road near the frontier fortresses. There was a little runnel running underneath the road, conveying a mountain stream ; it was arched with great care, and the arch was made of good hewn stone well smoothed. But when we came right on to this road we found something more astonishing still : we found that it was but the simulacrum or ghost of a road. It was not metalled ; it was but the plan or trace or idea of a road. No horses had ever trod its soft earth, no wheels had ever made a rut in it. It had not been used at all. Grass covered it. The explanation of this astonishing sight we did not receive until we had spoken in their own tongue the next day to the imperturbable Andorrans.

It was as though a school of engineers had been turned on here for fun, to practise the designing of a road in a place where land was valueless, upon the very summit of the world.

We two men, however, reasoned thus (and reasoned rightly as it turned out) :

"The tall and silent Andorrans in a fit of energy must have begun this road, though later in another fit they abandoned it. Therefore it will lead towards their country."

And as we were very tired of walking up a steep which had now lasted for so many hours, we determined to follow the large zigzags of this unknown and magic half-road, and so we did.

It was the oddest sensation in the world walking in the mist a mile and more above the habitations of men, upon unmetalled, common earth which yet had the exact shape of pavements, cuttings, and embankments upon either side, with no sort of clue as to where it led or as to why men began to make it, and still less of an argument as to why they had ceased.

It went up and up in great long turns and z's upon the face of the mountain, until at last it grew less steep; the mist grew colder, and after a long flat I thought the land began to fall a little, and I said to my companion :

" We are over the watershed, and beneath us, miles beneath us, are the Andorrans."

When by the continuance of the fall of the land we were certain of this we took off our hats, in spite of the fog which still hung round us very wet and very cold and quite silent, and expected any moment a revelation.

We were not disappointed. Indeed, this attitude of the mind is never disappointed. Without a moment's warning the air all round us turned quite bright and warm, a strong gust blew through the whirling vapour, and we saw through the veil of it the image of the sun. In a moment his full disc and warmth was on us. The clouds were torn up above us ; the air was immediately quite clear, and we saw before us, stamped suddenly upon the sight, a hundred miles of the Pyrenees.

They say that everything is in the mind. If that be true, then he and I saw in that moment a country which was never yet on earth, for it was a country which our minds had not yet conceived to be possible, and it was as new as though we had seen it after the disembodiment of the soul.

The evening sun from over Spain shone warm and low, and every conceivable colour of the purples and the browns filled up the mountain tangle, so that the marvel appeared as though it had been painted carefully in a minute way by a man's hand; but the colours were filled with light, and so to fill colour with light is what art can never do. The main range ran out upon either side, and the foot-hills in long series of peaks and ridges fell beneath it, until, beyond, in what might have been sky or might have been earth, was the haze of the plains of Ebro.

"It is no wonder," said I to my companion, "that the Andorrans jealously preserve their land and have refused to complete this road."

When I had said that we went down the mountain side. The lower our steps fell the more we found the wealth and the happiness of men. At last walls and ploughed land appeared. The fields grew deep, the trees more sturdy, and under the shelter of peaks with which we had just been acquainted, but which after an hour or so of descent seemed hopelessly above us, ran rivers which were already tamed and put to a use. One could see mills standing upon them. So we went down and down.

There is no rejuvenescence like this entry into Andorra, and there is no other experience of the same sort, not even the finding of spring land after a month of winter sea : that vision of brilliant fields coming down to meet one after the endless grey waste of the sea.

It was, I tell you again, a country completely new, and it might have been of another world, much better than our own.

So we came at last to the level of the valley, and the first thing we saw was a pig, and the second was a child, and the third was a woman. The pig ran at us : for he was lean. The child at first smiled at us because we were human beings, and then divining that we were fiends who had violated his sacred home began to cry. The woman drove the pig from us and took in the child, and in great loneliness and very sad to be so received we went until we should find men and citizens, and these we found of our own size, upstanding and very dignified, and recognised them at once to be of the wealthy and reserved Andorrans. It was clear by their faces that the *lingua franca* was well known to them, so I said to the first in this universal tongue :

"Sir, what is the name of this village ? "

And he replied : " It is Saldeu." But this he

199

said in his own language, which is somewhat more difficult to understand than the *lingua franca.*

"I take it, therefore," said I, "that I am in the famous country of Andorra."

To which he replied: "You are not many miles from the very town itself: you approach Andorra 'the Old.'"

The meaning of this I did not at first exactly understand, but as we went on, the sun having now set, I said to my companion: "Were not those epithets right which we attached to the Andorrans in our fancy before we attempted these enormous hills? Were we not right to call them the smiling and the tall Andorrans?"

"You are right," he answered to me, thinking carefully over every word that he said. "To call them the secluded and the honourable Andorrans is to describe them in a few words."

We then continued our way down the darkening valley, whistling little English songs.

The Barber   ❧   ❧   ❧   ❧   ❧

HUMANITY, my dear little human race, is at once more difficult to get at and more generally present than you seem to know. You are yourselves human beings, dear people. Yet how many have so fully understood their fellows (that is, themselves) that they could exactly say how any man will behave or why any man behaves as he does? But with that I am not to-day concerned. I am concerned with another matter, which is the impossibility of getting away from these brothers of ours, even if we desire to do so.

Note you here, humans, that in reality you do not, even the richest of you, try to get away from your brothers. You do not like solitudes; you like sham, theatrical solitudes. You like the Highlands on condition that you have driven away the people rooted there, but also on condition that you may have there the wine called champagne. Now if you had seen that wine made, the gathering of the apples in the orchards of the Rhine and the Moselle, the adding of the sugar, the watching of the fermentation, and the corking with a curious machine, you would appreciate that if you insist upon champagne in the Highlands, then you are certainly taking humanity with you. If you could follow the thing farther and see them all passing the stuff on, each a little afraid of being found out, then you would know that as you drank your champagne in the most solitary valley you had done far from getting rid of humanity. All the grotesque of man and all his jollity, all his stupidity and all his sin, went with you into your hermitage and it would have gone with you anyhow without the champagne. You cannot make a desert except by staying away from it yourself. All of which leads me to the Barber.

First, then, to give you the true framework of that astonishing man. For exactly thirty-six hours there had been nothing at all in the way of men; and if thirty-six hours seems but a short time to you as you read it, it certainly was a mighty long time for me who am writing this. Of those thirty-six hours the first few had been enlivened (that is, from five in the morning till about noon) with the sight of a properly made road, of worked stone, of mown grass, and of all that my fellow beings are busily at throughout the world. For though I had not seen a man, yet the marks of men were all around, and at last as I went into the Uplands I bade farewell to my kind in the shape of an old rusty pair of rails still united by little iron sleepers, one link of a Decauville railway which a generation before had led to a now abandoned mine.

My way over the mountains lay up a gulley which

turned as unexpectedly as might the street of a mediæval town; and which was quite as narrow and as enwalled as the street of any city; but instead of houses there were ugly rocks, and instead of people very probably viewless devils. Still, though I hated to be away from men I went on because I desired to cross the high ridge which separated me from a dear pastoral people, of whom I had heard from poets and of whom I had read in old books. They were a democracy simple and austere, though a little given to thieving, and every man was a master of his house and a citizen within the State. This curious little place I determined to see, though the approach to it was difficult. There are many such in Europe, but this one lies peculiarly alone, and is respected, and I might say in a sense worshipped, by the powerful Government to which it is nominally subject.

Well, then, I went on up over the ridge and, by that common trick of mountains, the great height and the very long way somehow missed me; it grew dark before I was aware, and when I could have sworn I was about four thousand feet up I was close upon eight thousand. I had hoped to manage the Farther Valleys before nightfall, but when I found it was impossible what I did was this: I scrambled down the first four or five hundred feet of the far side before it was quite dark, until I came to the beginnings of a stream that leapt from ledge to ledge. It was not large enough to supply a cottage

On Everything

well, but it would do to camp by, for all one needs
is water, and there was a little brushwood to burn.
Next morning with the first of the light I went on
my scramble downwards—and it was the old story
(which everyone who has wandered in the great
mountains of Europe knows so well), I was in the
Wrong Valley. I was used to that sort of thing, and
I recognised the signs of it at once. I made up my
mind for a good day's effort, which, when one is by
oneself, is an exasperating thing ; I tried to guess
from my map what sort of error I had made (and
failed). I knew that if I followed running water I
should come at last to men. At about three o'clock
in the afternoon I made a good meal of stale bread,
wine, and my companion the torrent, which had now
grown to be a sort of river and made as much noise
as though it were a politician. Then I thought I
would sleep a little, and did so (you must excuse so
many details, they are all necessary). It was five
when I rose and took up my journey again. I
shouldered the pack and stolidly determined that
another night out in these warmer lowlands would
not hurt me, when I saw something which is quite
unmistakable upon the grass of those particular
hills, a worn patch, and another worn patch a yard
or two ahead. That meant a road, and a road
means men—sooner or later.

Sure enough, within half a mile, the worn patches
having become now almost continuous, I rounded
a big rock and there was a group of huts.

The Barber

There were perhaps two dozen of them, perhaps more. Three-quarters were built of great logs with large, very flat roofs over them held down by stones; one quarter were built of the same rough stones, and there was a tiny church of dirt colour, with two windows; and neither window had glass in it. I had found men. And I had found something more.

For as I went down the main street of this Polity (they had "Main Street" stuck up in their language at the corner of the only possible mud alley of their town) I saw that blessed sight which sings to the heart and is one of the thirteen signs of civilisation, a barber's pole. It was not very good; it was not planed or polished; the bark was still upon the chestnut wood of it; but there was a spiral of red round it in the orthodox fashion, at the end of it a tuft of red wool, and underneath it in very faded rough letters upon a board the words, "Here it is barbered." More was to follow. I confess that I desired to draw, for beyond the little huts the mountains, once dreadful, now, being so far above me, compelled my attention. But just as I had sat down upon a great stone to draw their outline, there appeared through the disgusting little door under the barber's pole one of those humans whom I have mentioned so often in these lines.

He was about thirty, but he had never known care; his complexion was pink and white, his eyes were lively, his brown hair was short curled, trimmed

and oily, and some fifteen degrees from the middle
of his head to the eastward went a very clear
white line which was the parting of his hair. His
two little moustaches curled upwards like rams'
horns; his chin was square and firm, but very full
and healthy. He was looking out for customers.
Oh, Humanity, my brothers, Divine Object of the
Positivists, Plaything of the Theologians, Food of the
God of War, Great of Destiny, Victim of Experience,
Doubtful of Doom, Foreknowing of Death, Humanity enslaved, exultant, always on the march, never
arriving, the only thing yet made that can laugh and
can cry, Humanity, in fine, which was generously
designed as matter for poets, hear! He was looking
out for customers! Even to the railways of his own
land it was nearly a hundred miles; no one read
print; beyond Latin no foreign language perhaps was
known. No vehicle on wheels had ever been into
that place, even the maps were wrong, no one therein
had seen a metalled road, a ship of any kind, nor
perhaps one polished stone. But he was looking
out for customers.

He spotted me. He used no subterfuge; he smiled
and beckoned with his finger, and I went at once, as
men do when the Figure appears at the Doorway of
the Feast and beckons some one of the revellers into
the darkness. I obeyed. He put a towel round my
neck; he lathered my chin; I gazed at the ceiling,
and he began to shave.

On the ceiling was an advertisement in the English

tongue. I am inured by this time to the inconceivable stupidity of modern commerce, but (as the
Pwca said to the Acorn) "the like of this I never
saw." There most certainly was not a man in the
whole place who had ever heard of the English
language, nor, I will bet a boot, had anyone been
there before me who did, at any rate not since the
pilgrimages stopped. Yet there was this advertisement staring me in the face, and what it told me to do
was to buy a certain kind of bicycle. It gave no
evidence in favour of the thing. It asserted. It
said that this bicycle was the best. There was a
picture of a young man riding on the bicycle, and
under it in very small letters in the language of the
country an address where such bicycles might be
bought. The address was in a town as far away as
Bristol is from Hull, and between it was range upon
range of mountains, and never a road.

I watched this advertisement, and the Barber all
the while talked to me of the things of this world.

He would have it that I was a stranger. He
mentioned the place—it was about eighty miles away
—from which I came. He said he knew it at once
by my accent and my hesitation over their tongue.
He asked me questions upon the politics of the place,
and when I could not reply he assured me that he
meant no harm ; he knew that politics were not to
be discussed among gentlemen. He recommended
to me what barbers always recommend, and I saw
that his bottles were from the ends of the earth—

some French, some German, some American—at least their labels were. Then when he had shaved me he very politely began to whistle a tune.

It was a music-hall tune. I had heard it first eighteen months before in Glasgow, but it had come there from New York. It was already beginning to be stale in London—it did not seem very new to the Barber, for he whistled it with thorough knowledge, and he added trills and voluntary passages of merit and originality. I asked him how much there was to pay. He named so considerable a sum that I looked at him doubtfully, but he still smiled, and I paid him.

I asked him next how far it might be to the next village down the valley. He said three hours. I went on, and found that he had spoken the truth.

In that next village I slept, and I went forward all the next day and half the next before I came to what you would call a town. But all the while the Barber remained in my mind. There are people like this all over the world, even on the edges of eternity. How can one ever be lonely?

On High Places ∽ ∽ ∽ ∽ ∽

ALL over the world every kind of man has had for the high places of his country, or for the high places that he has seen in travel (though these last have made upon him a lesser impression), a sentiment closely allied to religion and difficult to fit in with common words. It is upon such sites that sacrifice upon special occasion has been offered. It is here that you will find rare, unvisited, but very holy shrines to-day, and even in its last and most degraded form the men of our modern societies, who are atrophied in such things, spur themselves to a special emotion by distant voyages in which they can satisfy this adoration of a summit over a plain. It is not capable of analysis; but how marvellously it fills the mind. It is not difficult to understand that monk of the Dark Ages—to be accurate, of the early eleventh century—who, having doubtless seen Paris a hundred times from the height of Montmartre, could not believe that the martyrdom of St. Denis had taken place on the plain. Something primal in him demanded the high and lonely place as the scene of the foundation of the Church of Lutetia, and he would have it that St. Denis was martyred there. All the popular stories were with him, and the legend arose. Up and down Europe, wherever

there are hills, you will find upon conspicuous crags
or little peaks, upon the loneliest ridges, a chapel.
There is one such on a hill near Remiremont; there
is another at Roncesvalles; there is another on the
high platform at Portofino; there is another on the
very height called Holy Cross above Urgel. In its
way, St. Martha's in Surrey is of that kind. There
are hundreds everywhere throughout Christendom,
and they witness to this need of man for which, I
say, there is no name.

I have heard of a mountain in Ireland, in the west
of that country, to the summit of which upon a
certain day of the year the people and the priests will
go together, and Mass will be said in the open air
upon that height. And so it is in several places of
the Vosges and of the Pyrenees, and in one or two,
I believe, of the foothills of the Alps. Everywhere
men associate the exaltation of the high places with
worship.

It is to be noticed that where men cannot satisfy
this emotion by the spectacle of distant hills, or by
the presence of nearer ones which they can climb
upon occasion, they remedy the defect either in their
architecture or with their trees. The people of
Northern France lacked height in their landscape,
and in their forests the trees were neither of the sort
nor stature which commonly satisfy the need of which
I speak. Their architecture supplies it. It has
reached its most tremendous expression in Beauvais,
its most stately in Flanders. No man well under-

stands what height can be in architecture unless he
has watched one of the great Flemish steeples from
a vantage point upon another. They are sufficiently
amazing when you see them, as they were meant to
be seen, from the flat pastures outside the city walls.
But where most you can appreciate the way in which
they make up the impression of the Netherlands is
from a platform such as that of Delft, half way up
the tower just below the bells. You look out to an
horizon which is that of a misty sea, land absolutely
level, and here and there the line between earth and
sky is cut by these shafts of human effort whose
purpose it is—and they achieve it—to give high
places to a plain. So also Strasburg stands up in
that great river plain of which it is the centre, and
so Salisbury towers above the central upland of
South England. And so Chichester over the deep
loam of the sea plain of Sussex. You will further
note that as you approach the mountains this attempt
grows less in human effort, and is replaced by something else. At Bordeaux on the great flat sweep of
the river, with the level vineyards all round about,
you have a mighty spire, sprung probably from
English effort and looking down the river as a land-
mark and a feature in the sky. But close against
the Pyrenees, nay when, two days' walking south of
the city, you first begin to see those mountains,
height fails you in architecture. You have not got
it at Dax, nor in the splendid and deserted aisles of
Auch, nor in the complicated detail of St Bertrand;

nor is there any example of it in Perpignan ; but at Narbonne again, where what you have to look at are the flat approaches of the sea, height comes in in a peculiar way ; it is the height not of towers, but of walls. It has been remarked by many that effect of this kind is lacking in Italy ; but in Italy, wherever you may be, you have the mountains. South of the Sierra Guadarama there in no attempt to diversify the line of the horizon in this fashion. There is nothing in Madrid to which a man looks up in order to satisfy this need for the high places, nor in the churches of the villages round about. The millions spent upon the Escorial were spent with no such object ; but then, south of those mountains, the range stands up in a steep escarpment and everywhere is master of the plain. To the North, where they sink away more gradually and form no crest upon which the eye can repose, at once man supplies for himself the uplifting of the face which his soul must have, and the glorious vision of Segovia is proof of it. The castle and the cathedral of that famous city are like a tall ship riding out to sea ; or they are like a man preaching from a rock with uplifted hands ; or they are like the miraculous appearance of some divine messenger standing facing one above the steeps of the hill.

It is so in all the places I can remember ; it is so in the Valley of the Ebro, where Saragossa raises a tall nave and the tall columns of the Pilar, whereas, if you go northward and begin to see the

hills this feature fails. It is not apparent in Huesca
Jaca, right under the High Pyrenees, has none of it.
I can remember exceptions; one place, among the
most famous in Europe, which was built for a mountain
kingdom and under the influence of mountaineers,
though it stands in a plain. And that is Brou,
which seems to be made for mountains rather than
for the plain. And there are many modern errors
in the matter due to the copying of some style
pedantically and to the absence of native inspiration. The chief of these is Lourdes, whose hideous
basilica ought never to have attempted height in
the midst of those solemn hills. But the history of
man when he is dealing with his shrines is a history
of perpetual betterment, and some day Lourdes will
be replaced by a much worthier thing. The crypt
is already excellent, and many good changes in
European building have begun with the crypt.
There are errors, I say, of this sort due to the
modern divorce between personality and production,
and there are accidents, though rare, like that of
Brou, where a mountain building is set in a plain,
though hardly ever a building of the plains in the
mountains. But for the most part, and taking
Europe as a whole, the rule holds good. Consider
the church called L'Epine. It is not high, but every
line of it is designed to give the effect of height,
and the farther you are from it the more it seems
to soar, and the greyer it gets the more finely is it
drawn upwards. It stands in the roll of those vast

213

Catalaunian plains where twice the fate of Europe
has been decided; where first Attila was rolled backwards, and where more than a thousand years after
the armies destined to destroy the Revolution failed.
It is the mark and the centre of that plain.   But as
you get towards the Mountain of Rheims on the
north, the Argonne upon the east, the note of height
in stone is withdrawn.   The Argonne is low, the
Mountain of Rheims, though high and noble, is
hardly a true mountain, but each uplifts the face.

Among the many misfortunes of men confined to
this island, in the great cities of it, it may be counted
a good fortune that they have, more than most men
bound by modern industry, the opportunity of the
high places.   Lancashire especially has them at its
doors, and anyone who will talk much to Lancashire
folk will find how greatly the presence of the moors
still enters into their lives.   Notably is this true of
the Peak just to the east of the great industrial
plain, and the sense of height and the satisfaction of it is perhaps nowhere more splendidly met
than by the spectacle of that plain beneath a winter sunset as one sees it from the height of the road
above Glossop, if it be a Sunday evening when the
smoke is not dense, because for twenty-four hours
the factories have been silent.   The smoke then
hangs in wreaths like light clouds against the sunset
and one perceives in a very marvellous and sudden
fashion beneath one the life of industrial England.
It is an aspect of the country not easily forgotten.

On High Places

And everywhere Englishmen have presented to them
this effect of height within a smaller compass than
the men of other European nations. For in the
other nations men are either of the mountains or
of the plains. But here the isolated and numerous
masses of old rocks in Wales, in Cumberland, and
just north of the Midlands, and the sharp escarp-
ments of the five ranges of the chalk that radiate
from Salisbury Plain, and the isolated ridge of the
Malverns, and the wall of the Cotswolds over the
Vale of Severn, make it so that nearly all those who
live on this island, and especially those who live
in the busiest part of it, have their line of hills
before them. East Anglia and the Fens are an
exception, and much of the Valley of the Thames
as well. And here comes in the lack of London
London has no high places. It is the chief mis
fortune in the aspect of the city. It was not always
so. Popular instinct was very powerful here. Since
the Surrey hills had not their escarpment turned
towards the Thames, and since looking nowhere
round could the Londoner get height, he made it
for himself, and the Gothic London of the Middle
Ages was a mass of spires, chief and glorious above
which was the highest spire in all Europe, higher than
Strasburg and higher than Cologne, old St. Paul's.
It stood up on its hill above the river, and gave
unity to all that scheme of spires below. Neglect
began the ruin, the Great Fire did the rest, and
height in London has disappeared. The tall houses

and narrow gorges of streets that are the characteristic of Paris and of Edinburgh are unknown to London. Here and there the sense of which I speak is satisfied. Coming up Ludgate Hill, for instance, and seeing the mass of St. Paul's above it, or in one place where, as you come out of a narrow Westminster street, the upshooting of the repetitive lines of Victoria Tower suddenly strike you. But as a whole height is lacking here. Nor in so vast a place, now fixed in certain traditions, can it be supplied. It is a pity.

On Some Little Horses 〜 〜 〜

ALL the upland was full of little horses, little ponies of the upland. They looked with curious and interested eyes at man, but none of them had known his command. When men passed them riding they saw that there was some alliance between men and their brothers, and they asked news of it. Then they bent their heads down again soberly, to graze on the new pasture, and the wind blew through their manes and their tails; they were happy beasts, thinking of nothing, and knowing nothing but themselves, yet in their movements and the look of their eyes one could see what the skies were round them, and what the world—they were so much a part of it all.

In the hollows of the forest there were not many birds, not nearly as many as one had heard in the Weald, but one great hawk circled up in spirals against the wind. The wind was blowing splendidly through an air quite blue and clear for many miles, and growing clearer as the afternoon advanced in gladness. It was a sea wind that had been a gale the day before, but during the night everything had changed in South England, and the principal date of the year was passed, the date which is the true beginning of the year. The mist of the morning had scudded before thick Atlantic weather ; by noon it was lifted into clouds, by mid-afternoon those clouds were large, heralding clouds of Spring against an unbounded capacity of sky. There was no longer any struggle between them and the gale ; they went together in procession over the country and towards the east.

The ridges of the land, like great waves, rolled in also from the westward ; they were clearer and they were sharper with every hour, until at last the points of white chalk pits upon hills a day's ride away showed clearly under the sunlight, and a man could see the trees even upon the horizon line.

The water that one passed in the long ride seemed to grow clearer, and the woods to have more echoes. Then, whatever in the mind turned to memory, as the mind of all men does in Spring when they have done with their own springtime, turned to memory transformed and was full of visions ; and whatever of the mind turned to the future, as most of the mind must do in men of any age when the vigour of the Almighty is abroad, looked at it through a veil which was magical.

It seemed as though under the growing sunlight the change that had come, the touch, the spell, was a thing appreciable in moments of time and growing as one watched. You would have said that all the forest was wakening. The flowers you would have said, and especially the daffodils, had just broken

On Some Little Horses

from the bud, and evergreens that had been in leaf all winter you would have said had somehow put on a new green. The movement of the wind in the branches of the beeches did not seem to move them but to find a movement responding to its own, and the colour of those branches against the blue sky and touched by the sun as it grew low was full of vivid promise. If it be not too much to ascribe a mood to all inanimate and animate things, there was a mood about one which was a complete forgetfulness of decay, a sort of trampling upon it, a rising out of it, and a using of it into life : a using of it up into life.

Over three ridges of land to the southward lay the sea. When the sea is in movement before a clear wind that is not a storm, and under a clear, sharp sky, its movement may be perceived for miles and miles. No one can see the waves, but the distant belt is shot with a pattern which one feels so far as the eye commands it, and that belt is alive, and it is a moving thing. Moreover, the high sea downs, the great chalk lifts of that shore of the world, are different on such days from what they are upon any others, and receive life from the sea that made them. All that world upon that morning you would have said was not only receiving gifts from the sea, but was itself apparently born from the sea, lived by the air of it, and had been engendered in the depths of it before ever men were on earth.

And of the sea also were the little horses.

On Everything

When the Spring took them they would suddenly gallop forward without any purpose beyond their wanton pleasure, and arch their necks towards the ground, and bound as a wave bounds; or they would go together, first one starting, then a comrade, then half a dozen of the herd, with a short but easy gait which exactly recalled the movement of salt water under the call of the wind: the movement of salt water where the deeps are, following and following and following, before it rises to break upon the shallows, or to turn back on its course along the eddies of hidden streams.

Anyone seeing the little horses was ready to believe that they had come from the Channel and not from the land at all, but that divine mares had bred them which moved over the tops of the waves, and that their sires flew invisibly along with the south-west wind. The heather bent a little beneath their rapid raids, and when they swerved, halted, and lifted up their heads to let the breeze blow out their manes, then they became, even more thoroughly than before, things of the Channel and of the bowling air. They were full of gladness.

The little horses did not know that they were owned by men; and if now and then men gave them food in the cold weather, or now and then saw to the housing of them, or now and then marked them with a mark, a short, forgotten pain, all these things they took like any other brief and passing

On Some Little Horses

accidents of fate. It was not man that had made
their home, nor man that ordered the things they
saw and used. They had not in anything about
them that look which animals have when they have
learned that man is of all things upon earth the
fullest of sorrow, nor that which beasts have, when
they have seen in man, without understanding it, what
a principal poet has called "the hideous secret of
his mirth"—though "hideous" is an unfair word,
for the secret sorrow of man is closely allied with
something Divine in his destiny. Such beasts as
are continually the companions of our souls and of
whom another poet has said that they are "subject
and dear to man," take from him invariably something of his foreknowledge of death. And you may
see in the patient oxen of the mountains and even
in the herded sheep of the Downs something of
man's burden as they take their lives along. But
most you will see what price is paid by those who
accompany us when you watch dogs and find that,
apart from the body, they can suffer, as we can
suffer, and sometimes suffer to the death. So dogs
that have known men know loneliness also, and
make, as men make, for distant lights at night, and
are not happy without living homes. Two things
only they have not, which are speech and laughter
And those animals which men deal with continually
come also into an easy or an uneasy subservience to
him, and you may note their hesitation where there
is an unaccustomed duty, and you may note their

beginnings of panic when men are not there to decide some difficult thing for them.

These little horses of which I write had as yet known none of these things, and anyone who looked at them closely could see what it was that the saints meant by "innocence in Nature." There was no evil in them at all, and the good that was in them was a simple good, of the earth and of the place in which they lived. There, away northward, it was the Downs; eastward and westward, the Forest; southward, under the sunlight, the Sea. That was all the little horses knew; and the man who in such a place and at that moment in the springtime could remember nothing more was very much more blessed than any other of his kind. But later he must remember Acheron; and what he will bear beyond Acheron—the consequence of things done.

Not so the Little Horses.

On Streams and Rivers   ∾   ∾   ∾

THERE is a pass called the Bon Agua, and also Bon Aigo, which leads from the heights of the Catalans to those other heights of Aragon, or as some would say of Bearn, for the pass is from the south of the mountains to the north; on the northern side one knows why it is called Bon Agua, because one sees many thousands of feet below one the little bracelet, the little chain, of the young Garonne.

Do not mistake me, there are two sources of the Garonne. That which is most famous does the most famous thing; for it rises on the far side of the mountains and it plunges into a pond, quite a little pond. Then it cascades underground, through dark passages of which no one knows anything, and comes out beyond the main chain of the hills to join its other quieter sister from the Bon Agua. This startling source, I say, is the most famous, because it does the most startling things, though not more wonderful than what a Yorkshire river does, for there is a Yorkshire river in the West Riding which runs into the pond called Mallam Tarn and reappears afterwards beyond a rocky ridge; but this Garonne of which I speak goes right under high and silent mountains where there

223

are no men, and this is a feat performed, I think, by
no other river, not even by the Rhone, which also is
lost for the time underground (though few people
know it), nor by the River Mole, which plays at
being lost and never quite is, and certainly has not
the courage to attempt the tunnelling of any hill,
though it is proud to be called the "snouzling
Mole," which, by the way, it was first called in the
year 1903—but I digress, and I must return to the
Bon Agua.

Well, then, there I say under the Bon Agua runs
the quieter of the two streams which unite in the
Val D'Aran to form the Garonne, and there it was
that a companion of mine seeing that little stream
looked at it with profound sadness, and said—the
things which shall be the text of what I have to say
here. For he said :

"Poor little Garonne ! Innocent and lovely little
Garonne ! I have never seen a stream so small, nor
so pure, nor so young, nor so far from men. But
you are on your way to things you do not know.
For first of all you will join that boasting sister of
yours which has come from under the hills, and can
talk of nothing else ; and then you will go past the
King's Bridge being no longer among kind and
silent Spaniards, and you will . have entered the
territory of the Republic which is fierce and evil,
and you will grow greater and wider and not more
happy until you will come to the perfectly detestable town of Toulouse. . . . Thence after you will

have no pleasure, but only a certain grandeur to be passing through the Gascon fields, and all your desire will be for the sea in which at last you shall merge and be lost. And so strong will be your desire for that dissolution that you will be willing to mix your name with another name, to marry the Dordogne, and then you will die and you will be glad of it."

This is the way my friend spoke to the Garonne when he saw it first rising in the hills. He did not sing it as he might have sung it, the song it best likes to hear, which is called, "Had the Garonne but wished!" Nor did he try to console it with any flap-doodle about the common lot of rivers, knowing well that some rivers were happier and some less happy. But he spoke to the Garonne as to something that could hear and know. Now this is what men have always done to rivers.

It is in this way that rivers have acquired names, not only among men but among gods; and it is in this way that they convey a fate to the countrysides of which they are the souls.

There is no country of which this is more true than it is true of England. Englishmen of this time—or at least of the time just past—perpetually and rightly complained that somehow or other they missed themselves. Some took refuge in a dream of a sort of a mystical England which was not there. Others reposed in the idea of an older England which may once have been; others, more foolish, hoped to find England again in something overseas. None of these would have suffered their error had they learnt England down English waters, seeing the great memories of England reflected in the English rivers, and meeting them in the silence and the perfection of the streams. But our roads first, and then our railways, our commerce which is from ports, and which must go direct towards them, our life, which is now in vast cities independent of streams, has made us neglect these things.

Consider such a list as this : Arundel when you see it as you come up Arun on the full flood tide. Chichester as you see it on the flood tide from Chichester harbour. Durham as you see it coming down under that cliff with the Cathedral as massive as the rock. Chester as you see it, sailing up the Dee with a light north wind from the sea. Gloucester as you see it from the Severn. Or Winchester as you pull, if you can pull, or paddle which is easier, against the clear and violent thrust of the Itchin. Canterbury as you see it from above or from below, upon the easy water of the Stour; and Lincoln as you see it from its little ditch—and I wonder how many men now journey up in any fashion from Boston ! So Norwich from the Yare. So Bramber for that matter from a place where the Adur grows narrow ; and what a sight Bramber must have been when the Castle stood whole upon the hill, physically blocking the advance into the Weald.

There is only one stream left, the Thames, which

we still know, and we very rightly know it; but we love it only for giving us one experience which we might, if we chose, repeat up and down England everywhere. There is no country in the world like this for rivers. The tide pushes up them to the very Midlands, from every sea. There is nothing of the history of England but is on a river, and as England is an island of birds, so is it more truly an island of rivers. Consider the River Eden, which is so difficult to descend; the Wiltshire Avon and the Hampshire Avon, and those little branch streams the Thame, the Cherwell, and the Evenlode.

Best of all, I think, as a memory or an experience is the Ouse, which runs from Bedford to the Wash, and has upon it the astonishing monument of Ely. Here is a river which no one can descend without feeling as he descends it the change of English provinces from the Midlands to the sea. He should start at Bedford; then he will pass through fields where tall elms give to the plains something more than could be given them by distant hills. The river runs between banks of deep grass in summer. It is contented everywhere; and as you go you are in the middle of a thousand years. You pass villages that have not changed; you carry your boat over weirs where there are mills, always shaded by large trees. Once in a day, at the most, you find an unchanging town: Huntingdon is such an one, or St. Ives, where I do believe the people are kinder than in any other town. Then, as you still go on, the land takes on another character. You begin to know that England is not only rich and full of fields but also was made by the sea. For you come to great flats—and that rather suddenly—where, as at sea, the sky is your contemplation. You notice the light, the colour, and the shapes of clouds. The birds that wheel and scream over these spaces seem to be sea-birds. You expect at any moment to hear beyond the dead line of the horizon the sound of surf and to see the glint of live water. Above such a waste rises, on what is called "an island," and is in truth "an island," the superb strength of Ely.

No one has seen Ely who has not seen it from the Ouse. It is a hill upon a hill, and now permanently present in the midst of loneliness. It is something made with a framework all around of accidental marsh and emptiness. Thenceafter the Ouse goes on. You get through and down the deep step of a lock, and beyond it is the salt water and busy energy that comes and goes from the sea. Very deep banks, alive with the salt and the swirl of the tide, shut in the boat for miles, and there are very high bridges uniting village to village above one, till at last the whole thing broadens, and one sees under the sunlight the roofs and the spars of King's Lynn; and, if one has no misadventure, one ends the journey at some narrow quay at a narrow lane of that delightful port and town.

There is one English river out of at least thirty

On Streams and Rivers

others. I wish that all were known! That journey down the Ouse is three days' journey—but it is such a slice of time and character and history as teaches you most you need know upon this Island. Only I warn anyone attempting it, let the boat be light and let it be shallow, and be ready to sleep in it; it is only thus that you can know an English river, and if you can draw, why it will be a greater pleasure. It is very cheap.

On Two Manuals   ❧   ❧   ❧   ❧

FLAUBERT, I believe, designed once to publish a Dictionary of Errors, and would actually have set about it had he not found the subject growing much too vast for any human pen. He also designed a reference book, or rather anthology, of follies, stupidities, rash judgments, and absurdities, but never lived to complete this great task. Now, reading this, I have wondered whether two little books might not be written which should prove useful severally to the undergraduate and to the politician. I do not say to the schoolboy, for no book yet written ever was or ever will be useful to him. But for the undergraduate a useful book might be written which I shall presently describe, and which would make a sort of foundation for all his studies. So also for the politician a second book might be written which should be of the greatest service. Let me now describe these two books. Perhaps among those who read this there will be so many men of leisure and learning as can in combination give the world the volumes I imagine.

The first book should be called "Modern Thought," and in this, without praise or blame and without any wandering into metaphysics or religion, the young fellow should be plainly taught to distinguish the

certain from the uncertain. I know of nothing in
which academic training just now is more at fault.
That training seems to consist in two branches.
First, the setting down of a very great number of
things each equally certain with the last and all
forming together one huge amorphic body or lump
of assertion; second, a whole sheaf of theories, the
whole fun of which consists in the fact that no one
of them can positively be proved but that all are
guesswork. These theories change from year to year,
and while they are defended with a passion astonish
ing to those who live in a larger world, there is no
pretence that they are true. The whole business
of them is quite obviously a game. Consider, for
instance, history. A lad is taught that William the
Conqueror won at Hastings in 1066; that the opinion
of the English people was behind the little wealthy
clique that put an end to the Stuarts; that London
heartily sympathised with the seven Bishops; that
all Parliamentary institutions grew up on the soil of
this island in the thirteenth century from Saxon
origins; and that four people called Hengist, and
Horsa, and Aella, and Cerdic led a great number of
Germans to various points of this Island, killed the
people living there and put the Germans in their
stead. Now of these assertions, all of which he is to
receive with equal certitude, all dogmatically affirmed,
all taught to him as brute bits of truth—some, as
that about Hastings, are rigidly true; some, such as
the attitude of London towards the seven Bishops,

are morally certain (though hardly capable of definite proof); some, as the weight of public opinion behind the Whigs, debatable though probable; some, like the Hengist and Horsa business, almost certainly mere legends—and so forth. It is to be noted that, if you are to teach at all, you must always have in your teaching some admixture of this error. No one can exactly balance the degree of probability attaching to each separate statement; there is no time to array all the evidence, and if there were, the mind of the student could not carry it. Each teacher, moreover, will have a scheme of values somewhat different from his neighbour's; but even if some admixture of the error I speak of be necessary, at least let the student be warned that it exists. For if he is not so warned one of two things will happen: either he will believe all he is told, with the most appalling results to himself, and, should he later become powerful, to the whole nation (we are seeing something of that in economics to-day), or he will (as the cleverer undergraduate usually does) become sceptical of all he hears; he will begin to wonder, having once found his teacher out in, let us say, the absurdity of pretending that Parliamentary institutions were peculiar to Britain, whether the Battle of Hastings were really fought in 1066 or no. When he has discovered, as any boy of education, travel, and common sense will discover, that the Normans were not Scandinavians, but Frenchmen, he will be led to reason that perhaps William the Conqueror never existed at all. This mood of universal scepticism is even more dangerous than that of bovine assurance, more dangerous to character, that is, and more dissolving of national strength.

As with the assertions so with the theories. There was a theory, for instance, that a tenure of land existed in ancient England by which this land was the common property of all, and was called the land of the "folk." Then this theory burst, and another theory swelled, which was that the "folk land" meant the land held by customary right as distinguished from land held by charter. Again, there was a theory that an original Saxon tendency to breed large landowners had gradually prevailed over feudal tenure. This theory burst, and another theory swelled, which was that the large units of land grew up by an accidental interpretation of Roman law.

In the book I propose all these theories could be very simply dealt with. The student should be warned that they are theories, and theories only, that their whole point and value is that they are not susceptible to positive proof; that what makes them amusing and interesting is the certitude that one can go on having a good quarrel about them, and the inner faith that when one is tired of them one can drop them without regret. Older men know this, but young men often do not, and they will take a theory in the Academies and make a friend of it, and at last, as it were, another self, and clasp it close to their souls and intertwine themselves with it, only to find towards thirty that they have been hugging a shade.

So much, then, for this first book. It would not need to be more than a little pocket volume of fifty or sixty pages, and a young man should have it to refer to at any moment of his studies. One of its maxims would be to look up the original evidence upon which anything he was told was based. Another rule he would find in it would be to underline all such words as "seems," "probably," and so forth, and watch in his books the way in which they gradually turn, as the argument proceeds, into "is" and "certainly." He would also be warned before reading the work of any authority to remember that that authority was a human being, to look up his biography, if possible to meet him personally, to find out what general knowledge he had and what impression he made upon the casual man that met him. How many men have written histories of a campaign and yet have been proved at a dinner-table ignorant of the range of artillery during their period! How many men have learnedly criticised the style of Rousseau upon a knowledge of French very much inferior to that of most governesses! I at Oxford knew a don who exposed and ridiculed the legend of the Girondins, but throughout his remarks pronounced their title with a hard *g*.

As for the politicians, their little guide-book through life should be of another sort. In this the first and most valuable part would deal with political judgment and prophecy. The utmost care would be taken by the author to show how valueless is any determination of the future, and how crass the mind which predicts with confidence. Since so very few men happen to have made lucky shots, it would be the peculiar care of the author in a loving manner to collect all the follies and misjudgments which these same men had made upon other grave matters. And, in general, the reader would be left very certain that every pompous prophecy he heard was a piece of folly. Next in the book would come examples of all that political men have said and done which they most particularly desired to have forgotten. This would serve a twofold purpose, for first it would amuse and instruct the politician as he read it, since the misfortunes of others are delightful to human kind, and, secondly, it would show him that he could not himself trust to the effect of time, and that his natural desire to turn his coat or to pretend to some policy he did not understand would at last be judged as it deserved. In the third and final portion of the book the politician would be given a list of interesting truths, with regard to the matter of his trade. It would be proved to him in a few sentences that his decisions depend upon various difficult branches oi study, and by a few suggested questions he would be convinced of his ignorance therein. The shortness of human life would be insisted upon, with examples showing how a man having painfully reached power was stricken with paralysis or died in torment. The ludicrous miscarriage of great plans would be laid before him, and, better still, the proof that the most successful adventures had proceeded almost entirely from chance, and surprised no one more than their authors.

At the end of the book would be a certain number of coupons permitting the reader to travel to many places which politicians commonly ignore, and there would be a list of the sights that he should see. As, for instance, the troops of such and such a nation upon the march, the artillery of such another at firing practice, and the opinion expressed by the populace in taverns in such and such a town. Then at the end would come a number of common phrases such as *cui bono, persona grata, toujours perdrix, double entendre, sturm und drang*, etc., with their English equivalents, if any, and their approximate meaning, when they possess a meaning. Upon the last page would be a list of the duties of a Christian man and a short guide to general conduct in conversation with the rich.

Armed with these manuals, the youth and manhood of a nation would at once and vastly change. You would find young men recently proceeded from the University filled with laudable doubts arising from the vastness of God's scheme, and yet modestly secure in certain essential truths such as their own existence and that of an objective universe, the voice of conscience, and the difference between right and wrong. While among those of more mature years, who were controlling the energies of the State, there would appear an exact observance of real things, an admitted inability to know what would happen fifty or even twenty years hence, and a habit of using plain language which they and their audience could easily understand; of using such language tersely, and occasionally with conviction.

But this revolution will not take place. The two books of which I speak will not be written. And if anyone doubts this, let him sit down and try to frame the scheme of one, and he will soon see that it is beyond any man's power.

On Fantastic Books ∽ ∽ ∽ ∽

THERE has fallen upon criticism since perhaps a century ago, and with increasing weight, a sort of gravity which is in great danger of becoming tomfoolery at last: as all gravity is in danger of becoming.

No one dares to discuss all that lighter thing which is the penumbra of letters, and, what is more, no man of letters dares to whisper that letters themselves are not often much more than a pastime to the reader, and are only very rarely upon a level with good and serious speculation: never upon a level with philosophy: still less upon a level with religion. It is perhaps even a mark of the eclipse of religion when any department of mere intellectual effort can raise itself as high as literature has raised itself in its own eyes; and since all expression now (or nearly all) is through the pen literature thus suffering from pride can impose its pride upon the world.

Two things alone correct this pride: first, that those who practise the trade of literature starve if they are austere or run into debt if they are not; secondly, that now and then one of the inner circle gives the thing away—for instance, Mr. Andrew

On Fantastic Books

Lang in his excellent and never-to-be-forgotten remarks delivered only last year at the dinner of the Royal Literary Fund. This Member of our Union said (with how much truth!) that the writers of stories should remember they were writers of stories and not teachers and preachers. And the same might be said to others of the Craft. If a man has had granted to him by the Higher Powers a jolly little lyric, why, that is a jolly little lyric. He should bow and scrape to those who gave it to him and hand it on to his fellow-men for a dollar. But it does not make him a god, and if it gives him so much as a swelled head it makes him intolerably wearisome. More tolerable are the victors of campaigns discussing at table their successes in the field than poets who forget their Muse: for to their Muse alone, or to those who sent her, do they owe what they are, as may very clearly be seen in the case of those whose Muse has deserted them and flown again up to her native heaven; nor is any case more distressing than that of ———.

All of which leads me to the Fantastic Books. One, two, a dozen at the most, in all the history of the world have ranked with the greatest. Rabelais is upon the summit, and the *Sentimental Journey* will live for some hundreds of years, but how many others are there which men remember? There is a sort of conspiracy against them led by the few intelligent vicious in league with the numerous

and virtuous fools; and thus the salt of the Fantastic
Books, which is as good as the salt of the sea, is
lost to the most of mankind.

Men sit in front of the writers of Fantastic Books
fair and squarely with their hands on their knees,
their eyes set, their mouths glum, their souls determined, and say:

"Come now, Fantastic Book, are you serious or
are you not serious?"

And when the Fantastic Book answers "I am
both."

Then the man gets up with a sigh and concludes
that it is neither. Yet the Fantastic Book was
right, and if people were only wise they would salt
all their libraries with Fantastic Books.

Note that the Fantastic Books are not of necessity jocose books or ribald books, nor even extravagant books. If I had meant to write about
extravagant books, *quâ* extravagant, you may be
certain I should have chosen that word. Rabelais
is extravagant and so is Sterne, but not on account
of their extravagance are they fantastic. The note
of the Fantastic Book is an easy escape from the
world. It is not imagination, though imagination
is a necessary spring to it: it is that faculty by
which the mind travels, as it reads, whether through
space or through time or through *quality*. A book is
a Fantastic Book, though time and space be commonplace enough, though the time be to-day and the
place Camberwell, if only the mind perpetually

On Fantastic Books

travels, seeing one after another unexpected things in the consequence of human action or in the juxtaposition of emotions.

There is a category of Fantastic Books most delightful, and never to my thinking overdone, which deals with journeys to worlds beyond the earth. I confess that I care nothing whether they are well written or ill written; so long as they are written in any language that I can understand I will read them; and to-day as I write I have before me a notable collection of such, every one of which I have read over and over again. I remember one called the *Anglo-Saxon Conquest of the Solar System* or words to that effect; another of a noble kind, called *Thuka of the Moon*. I only mention the two together by way of contrast; and I remember one in which somebody or other went to Mars and went mad, but I forget the title. Be they as well written as the *First Men in the Moon*, which is or will be a classic, or as ill written as a book which I may not mention because there is a law forbidding any one to tell unpleasant truths, so long as they concern voyages to the Planets they are worth reading.

Then, also, there is the future. The *Time Machine* is, perhaps, the chief of them; but writers who travel into the future, good or bad, are all delightful.

You may say that they are also always a little boring because they always try to teach a lesson or to prophesy. That is true, but when you have comforted yourself with the firm conviction that prophecies of this kind are invariably and wildly wrong the disturbance which they cause in your mind will disappear. I have among my most treasured books one of the early nineteenth century, called *Revelations of the Dead Alive*, in which the end of our age and its opinions upon *that* age are presented, and it is all wrong! But it is very entertaining all the same. Most ridiculous but not least entertaining of such books are the Socialist books, the books showing humanity in the future all Socialist and going on like sticks. There is, indeed, another type of mournful Socialist book much more real and much more troubling, in which Socialism has failed, and the mass of men go on like slaves; but no matter. A prophecy (when it is scientific) is always and invariably absolutely and totally wrong :—and a great comfort it is to remember *that!*

Yet another sort of Fantastic Book is your Journey to Hell or to Heaven. There is one I have read and re-read. It is called *The Outer Darkness*. I shall never cease to read it. It is a journey to a sort of Hell, and these are as a rule more entertaining than the Heavenly journey, though why I cannot tell. Does the same hold true of Dante?

Lastly, and much the most rare and much the most valued of all are the books which are fantastic, though they cling to the present and to things known. In these I would include imaginary people in the Islands and in the Arctic, and even those which introduce half-rational beasts. for such books

On Fantastic Books

depend for their character not upon the matter of the fantasy, but upon the manner. There is a book called *Ninety North*, for instance, which is all about a race of people at the North Pole, but the power of the book resides not in the distance of the scene, but in the vision of the writer and in the little irony that trickles down every page.

Who collects them or preserves them—the Fantastic Books? No one, I think. They are not catalogued under a separate Heading. They puzzle the writers of Indices; they bewilder Librarians. They must be grouted out of the mass of rubbish as Pigs in the Perigord grout out truffles. There is no other way.

Also, in the Perigord, truffles are hunted with Hounds.

The Unfortunate Man

TO all those who doubt the power of chance in human affairs; to all Stoics, Empiricists, Monists, Determinists, and all men whatsoever that terminate in this fashion, Greeting: Read what follows:

There was a man I used to know whose business it was to succeed in life, and who had made a profession of this from the age of nineteen. His father had left him a fortune of about £600 a year, which he still possesses, but, with that exception, he has been made by the gods a sort of puffball for their amusement, the sort of thing they throw about the room. It was before his father's death that a determination was taken to make him the land agent at the house of a cousin, who would give him a good salary, and it was arranged, as is the custom in that trade, that he should do nothing in return but dine, smoke, and ride about. The next step was easy He would be put into Parliament, and then, by quiet, effective speaking and continual voting, he would become a statesman, and so grow more and more famous, and succeed more and more, and marry into the fringes of one of the great families, and then die.

The Unfortunate Man

To this happy prospect was his future turned when he set out, not upon the old mare but upon the new Arab which his father had foolishly bought as an experiment, to visit his cousin's home and to make the last arrangements. And note in what follows that every step in the success-business came off, and yet somehow the sum total was disappointing, and at the present moment one can very definitely say that he has not succeeded.

He set out, I say, upon the new Arab, going gently along the sunken road that leads to the Downs, when a man carrying a faggot at the end of a pitchfork seemed to that stupid beast a preternatural apparition, and it shied forward and sideways like a knight's move, so that the Unfortunate Man fell off heavily and hurt himself dreadfully. When the Arab had done this it stood with its beautiful tail arched out, and its beautiful neck arched also, looking most pitifully at its fallen rider, and with a sadness in its eye like that of the horse in the Heliodorus. The Unfortunate Man got on again, feeling but a slight pain in the right shoulder. But what I would particularly have you know is this: that the pain has never wholly disappeared, and is perhaps a little worse now after twenty years than it has been at any previous time. Moreover, he has spent quite £350 in trying to have it cured, and he has gone to foreign watering-places, and has learnt all manner of names, how that according to one man it is rheumatism, and according to another it is suppressed gout, and according to another a lesion. But the point to him is the pain, and this endures.

Well, then, he rode over the Down and came out through the Combe to his cousin's house. The gate out of the field into the park was shut, and as he leaned over to open it he dropped his crop. I am ashamed to say that—it was the only act of the kind in his career, but men who desire to succeed ought not to act in this fashion—he did not get down to pick it up because he was afraid that if he did he might not be able to get on to the horse again. With infinite trouble, leaning right down over the horse's neck, he managed to open the gate with his hands, but in doing so he burst his collar, and he had to keep it more or less in place by putting down his chin in a ridiculous and affected attitude His hopes of making a fine entry at a pretty ambling trot, that perhaps his cousin would be watching from the window, were already sufficiently spoilt by the necessity he was under of keeping his collar thus, when the accursed animal bolted, and with the speed of lightning passed directly in front of a little lawn where his cousin, his cousin's wife, and their little child were seated admiring the summer's day. It was not until the horse had taken him nearly half a mile away that he got him right again, and so returned hot, dishevelled, and very miserable.

But they received him kindly, and his cousin's

The Unfortunate Man

wife, who was a most motherly woman, put him as best she could at his ease. She even got him another collar, knowing how terrible is the state of the soul when the collar is burst in company. And he sat down with them to make friends and discuss the future. He had always heard that among the chief avenues to success is to play with and be kind to the children of the Great, so he smiled in a winning manner at his cousin's little boy, and stretching out his arms took the child playfully by the hand. A piercing scream and a sharp kick upon the shin simultaneously informed him that he had fallen into yet another misfortune, and the boy's mother, though she was kindness itself, was startled into speaking to him very sharply, and telling him that the poor lad suffered from a deeply cut finger which was then but slowly healing. He made his apologies in a nervous but sincere manner, and in doing so was awkward enough to upset the little table which they had carried out upon the lawn, and upon which had been set the cups and saucers for tea. The whole thing was exceedingly annoying.

In this way did the Unfortunate Man enter the great arena of modern political life.

You must not imagine that he failed to obtain the sinecure which his father had sent him to secure. As I have already said, the failure of the Unfortunate Man was not a failure in major plans but in details. There may have been some to whom his career appeared enviable or even glorious, but Fate always watched him in a merry mood, and he was destined to suffer an interior misery which never failed to be sharpened and enlivened by the innumerable accidents of life.

He obtained for his cousin from the North of Scotland a man of sterling capacity, whose methods of agriculture had more than doubled the income of a previous employer; but as luck would have it this fellow, whose knowledge of farming was quite amazing, was not honest, and after some few months he had absconded with a considerable sum of money. A well which he had advised to be dug failed to find water for some two hundred feet, and then after all that expense fell in. He lamed one of his cousin's best horses by no fault of his own; the animal trod upon a hidden spike of wood and had to be shot; and in doing his duty by upbraiding a very frousty old man who was plunging about recklessly just where a lot of she (or hen) pheasants were sitting on their eggs he mortally offended the chief landowner of the neighbourhood, who was none other than the frousty old man himself, and who was tramping across the brushwood to see his cousin upon most important matters. It was therefore in a condition of despair that his cousin finally financed him for Parliament. The constituency which he bought after some negotiations was a corrupt seaport upon the coast of Rutlandshire (here is no libel!). He was at first assured that there would be no opposition, and acting upon this assurance took the one brief holiday which he had allowed himself for five years. The doctor, who was anxious about his nerves, recommended a sea voyage of a week upon a ship without wireless apparatus. He landed in Jamaica to receive a telegram which informed him that a local gentleman of vast influence, eccentric, and the chief landowner in the constituency, had determined to run against him, and which implored him to cable a considerable sum of money, though no such sum was at his disposal.

In the earthquake the next day he luckily escaped from bodily injury, but his nerves were terribly shaken. Thenceforward he suffered from little tricks of grimace which were to him infinitely painful, but to others always a source of secret, sometimes of open, merriment. He returned and fought the election. He was elected by a majority of 231, but not until he had been twice black-mailed, and had upon at least three occasions given money to men who afterwards turned out to have no vote. I may say, to put the matter briefly, that he retained the seat uninterruptedly until the last election, but always by tiny majorities at the expense of infinite energy, sweating blood, as it were, with anxiety at every poll, and this although he was opposed by the most various people. It was Fate!

He spoke frequently in the House of Commons, and always unsuccessfully, until one day a quite unexpected accident of war in a foreign country gave him his opportunity. It so happened that the

On Everything

Unfortunate Man knew all about this country; he
had read every book published upon it; it was the
one thing upon which he was an authority. And
ridiculous as had been his numerous efforts to engage
the attention of the august assembly, upon this
matter at least his judgment was eagerly expected.
The greatest courtesy was shown him, the Government arranged that he should speak at the most
telling time of the debate, and when he rose it was
before a full House, strained to an eager attention.

He struck an attitude at once impressive and
refined, stretched forth his hand in a manner that
gave promise of much to come, and was suddenly
seized with an immoderate fit of coughing. An
aged gentleman, a wool merchant by profession, who
sat immediately behind him, thought to do a kindly
thing by slapping him upon the back, being ignorant of that Shoulder Trouble with which the jolly
reader is acquainted. And the Unfortunate Man,
in the midst of his paroxysm of coughing, could not
restrain a loud cry of anguish. Confused inter-
ruptions, rising to a roar of protest, prevented him
from going further, and he was so imprudent, or
rather so wretchedly unlucky, as to be stung into
a violent expression of opinion directed towards
another member sitting upon his immediate left, a
money-lender by trade and very sensitive. This
fellow alone had heard the highly objectionable
word which the Unfortunate Man had let drop. It
is a word very commonly used by gentlemen in

The Unfortunate Man

privacy, but rare, indeed, or rather wholly unused
on the public occasions of our dignified political life.
In vain did those about the money-lender pull at his
skirts and implore him not to rise. He was white
with passion. He rose and appealed to the Chair.
He reiterated the offensive expression in the clearest
and most articulate fashion, apologising to the horri-
fied assembly for having to sully the air it breathed
by the necessary repetition of so abominable an
epithet, and he demanded the correction of the
monster in human form who had descended to use it.
The reprimand which the Unfortunate Man received
from the Chair was lengthy and severe, and from
that day forward he determined that the many
omens of ill-fortune which had marked his life had
reached their turn. He was too proud to resign,
but his caucus, in spite of further considerable gifts
of money, indignantly repudiated their Member,
and when the election came he had not the courage
to face it.

He is now living, broken and prematurely aged,
in a brick house which he has built for himself in a
charming part of the County of Surrey. He has
recently discovered that the title to his freehold
is insecure : an action is pending. Meanwhile, a
spring of water has broken out under the founda-
tions of the building, and some quarter of a mile
before its windows, obscuring the view of the
Weald in which he particularly delighted, a very
large factory with four tall chimneys is in process

of erection. These things have depressed him almost to the verge of despair, and he can only forget his miseries in motoring. He is continually fined for excessive speed, though by nature the most cautious of men, and terrified by high speeds, and I learn only to-day that as he was getting ready to go into Guildford to dispute a further fine before the Bench a backfire has put his wrist out of joint, and he suffers intolerable pain. *Militia est Vita Hominis!*

The Contented Man ◡ ◡ ◡ ◡

LUCIFER, for some time a bishop in Southern Italy (you did not know that, but it is true nevertheless, and you will find his name in the writings of Duchesne, and he took part in councils; nay, there was a time when I knew the very See of which he was bishop, but the passage of years effaces all these things)—Lucifer, I say, laid it down in his System of Morals that contentment was a virtue, and said that it could be aimed at and acquired positively, just as any other virtue can. Then there are others who have said that it was but a frame of mind and the result of several virtues; but these are the thinkers. The great mass of people are willing to say that contentment is strictly in proportion to the amount of money one may have, and they are wrong. I remember now there was a Sultan, or some such dignitary, in Spain, who counted the days of his life which had been filled with content, and found that they were seventeen. He was lucky; there are not many of us who can say the same. Then once a man told me this story about contentment, which seemed to me full of a profound meaning. It seems there was once an old gentleman who was possessed of something over half a million pounds, a banker, and this old gentleman every night of his life would go through certain little private books of his, compare them with the current list of prices, and estimate to a penny what he was worth before he slept. It was always a great pleasure to him to note the figures growing larger, and a great pain to him to note the rare occasions when they had shrunk a little in twenty-four hours. It so happened that this old gentleman lost a considerable sum of money which he had imprudently lent to a distant and foreign country too much praised in the newspapers, and he worried so much over the loss that he became ill and could not go to his office. His sons kept on the business for him, and every succeeding week they lost more and more of the money. But such was their filial piety that every night they gave the old gentleman false information, and that in some detail, so that he could put down his little rows of figures and see them growing larger night after night. You see, it was not the wealth that he desired, it was the increase in the little rows of figures; the wealth he consumed was the same; he wore the same clothes, he ate the same food, he lived in the same house as before, and he had for a companion eternally one or another of the two nurses provided by the doctor. The figures increasing regularly as they did filled him with a greater and a greater joy. After two years of this business he came to die, but his passing was a very happy one: he blessed his sons fervently and told them that

The Contented Man

nothing had more comforted his old age than their sober business sense; they had nearly doubled the family fortune during their short administration of it; he congratulated them and was now ready to go to his God in peace. Which he did, and two weeks after the petition in bankruptcy was presented by the young people themselves, always the more decent way of doing it: but the old man had died content.

Which parable leads up to the point at which I should have begun all this, which is, that once in my life, in the year 1901, during a heavy fog in the early morning of the month of November, in London, I met a perfectly contented man. He was the conductor of an omnibus. These vehicles depended in those days entirely on the traction of horses. They were therefore slow, and as the night, or rather the early morning, was foggy (it was a little after one) people going Westward—journalists for instance, who are compelled to be up at such hours—did not choose to travel in this way. There was no one in the 'bus but myself. I sat next the door as it rumbled along; there was one of those little faint oil lamps above it which are unique in Christendom for the small amount of light they give. It was impossible to read, but by the slight glimmer of it I saw suddenly revealed like a vision the face of that really happy man. It was a round face, framed in a somewhat slovenly hat and coat collar, but not slovenly in feature,

though not severe.   And as its owner clung to the
rail and swung with the movements of the 'bus he
whistled softly to himself a genial little air.   It was
not I but he that began the conversation.   He told
me that few things were a greater blessing in life
than gas fires, especially if one could regulate the
amount of gas by a penny in the slot.   He pointed
out to me that in this way there were never any
disputes as to the amount of gas used, and he also
said that it kept a man from the curse of credit,
which was the ruin of so many.   I told him that in
my house there was no gas, but that his description
almost made me wish there was.   And so it did,
for he went on to tell me how you could cook any
mortal thing with any degree of heat and at any
speed by the simple regulation of a tap.

It may be imagined how anxious I was on meeting so rare a being to go more deeply into the
matter and to find out on what such happiness reposed; but I did not know where to begin, because
there are always some questions which men do not
like asked, and unless one knows all about a man's
life one does not know what those questions are.
Luckily for me, he volunteered.   He told me that
he was married and had eight children.   He told
me his wages, which were astonishingly low, his
hours of labour, which were incredibly long, and he
further told me that on reaching the yard that
night he would have to walk a mile to his home.
He said he liked this, because it made him sleep,

and he added that in his profession the great difficulty was to get enough exercise. He told me how
often a day off was allowed him and how greatly he
enjoyed it. He told me the rent which he paid
for his two rooms, which appeared to be one-third
of his income, and congratulated himself upon the
cheapness and commodity of the place ; and so he
went on talking as we rumbled down the King's
Road, going farther and farther and farther West.
My day would end in a few hundred yards ; his not
for a mile or two more. Yet his content was far
the greater, and it affected me, I am sorry to say,
with wonder rather than with a similar emotion of
repose and pleasure.

The next part of his conversation discovered what
you will often find in the conversation of contented
men (or, rather, of partially contented men, for no
other absolutely contented man have I ever met
except this one), that is, a certain good-humoured
contempt for those who grumble. He told me that
the drivers of 'buses were never happy ; they had
all that life can give : high wages, fresh open-air
work, the dignity of controlling horses, and, what is
perhaps more important, ceaseless companionship,
for not only had they the companionship of chance
people who would come and sit on the front seats
of the 'bus outside, but they could and did make
appointments with friends who would come and ride
some part of the way and talk to them. Then,
again, as their work was more skilled, their tenure

of it was more secure, nor were they constrained
to shout "Liverpool Street" at the top of their
voices for hours on end, nor to say "Benk, Benk,
Benk" in imitation of the pom-pom. Nevertheless they grumbled. He was careful to tell me
that they were not really unhappy. What he
condemned in them was rather the habit and,
as it were, the fashion of grumbling. It seemed
as though no weather pleased them; it was always
either too hot or too cold; they took no pleasure
in the healthy English rain beating upon their
faces, and warm spring days seemed to put them
in a worse humour than ever. He condemned all
this in drivers.

When we had come to the corner of my street in
Chelsea as I got out I offered him a cigar which
I had upon me. He told me he did not smoke.
He was going on to tell me that he did not drink,
and would, I had no doubt, if he had had further
leisure, have told me his religion, his politics, and
much more about himself; but though the 'buses in
those days would wait very long at street corners
they would not wait for ever, and that particular
'bus rumbled and bumped away. I looked after it
a little wistfully, for fear that I might never see
a happy man again. And I walked down my street
towards my home more slowly than usual, thinking
upon the thing that I had just experienced.

I confess I found it a very difficult matter. That
experience not only challenged all that I had heard

The Contented Man

of happiness, but also re-awoke the insistent and
imperative question which men put to their gods
and which never receives an answer.   Ecstasy is
independent of all material conditions whatsoever.
That great sense of rectitude which so often em-
bitters men but permits them to support pain is
independent of material conditions also.   But these
are not contented moods : oblivion is ready to every
man's hand, and even the most unfortunate secure
a little sleep, and even the most tortured slaves
know that at last, for all the rules and fines and
regulations of the workshop, they cannot be forbidden to die ; but such a prospect is not equivalent
to content.   Further, there is a philosophy, rarely
achieved but conspicuous in every rank of fortune,
which so steadily regards all external accident as to
remain indifferent to the strain of living and even
to be, to some extent, master of physical pain.
But that philosophy, that mournful philosophy
which I have heard called "the permanent
religion of mankind," is not content: on the
contrary, it is very close indeed to despair.   It
is the philosophy of which the Roman Empire
perished.   It is the philosophy which, just because
it utterly failed to satisfy the heart of man, powerfully accelerated the triumph of the Church, as the
weight and pressure of water powerfully accelerate
the rise of a man's body through it, to the sunlight
and the air above, which are native and necessary to
him.   No, it was not the philosophy of the Stoics

which had laid a foundation for the 'bus-conductor's soul.

I could not explain that content of his in any way save upon the hypothesis that he was mad.

The Missioner ∾　∾　∾　∾　∾

IN one of those great halls which the winter
darkens and which are proper to the North, there
sat a group of men, kindly and full of the winter
night and of their food and drink, upon which for
many hours they had regaled together, and not only
full of song, but satiated with it, so long and so
loudly had they sung. They all claimed descent
from the Gods, but in varying degrees, and their
Chief was descended from the father of the Gods, by
no doubtful lineage, for it was his granfer's mother
to whom a witch in the woods had told the story
of her birth.

In the midst of them as they so sat, a large fire
smouldered, but having been long lit, sent up so
strong a shaft of rising air as drew all smoke with it,
towering to a sort of open cage upon the high roof
tree of that hall whence it could escape to heaven.

I say they were tired of song and filled with many
good things, but chiefly with companionship. They
had landed but recently from the sea; the noise
of the sea was in their ears as they so sat round the
fire, still talking low, and a Priest who was among
them refused to interpret the sound; but he said in
a manner that some mocked doubtfully, others heard

261

with awe, that the sea never sounded save upon nights when the Gods were abroad. He was the Priest of a lesser God, but he was known throughout the fleet of those pirate fishermen for his great skill in the interpretation of dreams, and he could tell by the surface of the water in the nightless midsummer where the shoals were to be found.

He said that on that night the Gods were abroad, and, indeed, the quality of the wind as it came down the gulf of the fjord provoked such a fancy, for it rose and fell as though by a volition, and sometimes one would have said that it was a quiet night, and, again, a moment after, one heard a noise like a voice round the corners of the great beams, and the wind pitied or appealed or called. Then a man who was a serf, but very skilled in woodwork, lying among the serfs in the outer ring beyond the fire in the straw, called up and said: "Lords, he is right; the Gods have come down from the Dovre-field; they are abroad. Let us bless our doors."

It was when he had so spoken that upon the main gate of that Hall (a large double engine of foot-thick pine swung upon hinges wrought many generations ago by the sons of the Gods) came a little knocking. It was a little tapping like the tapping of a bird. It rang musically of metal and of hollow metal; it moved them curiously, and a very young man who was of the blood said to his father: "Perhaps a God would warn us."

The keeper of the door was a huge and kindly

The Missioner

man, foolish but good for lifting, with whom by daylight children played, and who upon such evenings
lay silent and contented enough to hear his wittier
fellows. This serf rose from the straw and went to
unbar. But the Chief put his hand forward, and
bade him stay that they might still hear that little
tapping. Then he lowered his hand and the gate
was swung open.

Cold came with it for a moment, and the night
air ; light, and as though blown before that draught,
drifted into the hall a tall man, very young, who
bowed to them with a gesture they did not know,
and first asked in a tongue they could not tell,
whether any man might interpret for him.

Then one old man who was their pilot and who had
often run down into the vineyard lands, sometimes
for barter, sometimes for war, always for a wage, said
two words or three in that new tongue, hesitatingly.
His face was wrinkled and hard ; he had very bright
but very pale grey eyes that were full of humility.
He said three words of greeting which he had painfully learned twenty years before, from a priest, upon
the rocks of Brittany, who had also given him smooth
stones wherewith to pray ; and with these smooth
stones the old Pilot continually prayed sometimes to
the greater and sometimes to the lesser Gods. His
wife had died during the first war between Hrolf
and the Twin Brothers ; he had come home to find
her dead and sanctified, and, being Northern, he had
since been also a silent man. This Pilot, I say,

quoted the words of greeting in the strange tongue. Then the tall young stranger man advanced into the circle of the firelight and made a sign upon his head and his breast and his shoulders, which was like the sign of the Hammer of Thor, and yet which was not the sign of the Hammer of Thor. When he had done this, the Pilot attempted that same sign, but he failed at it, for it was many years since he had been taught it upon the Breton coast. He knew it to be magical and beneficent, and he was ashamed to fail.

The Chief of those who were descended from the Gods and were seated round the fire, turned to the Priest and said : " Is this a guest, a stranger sent, or is he a man come as an enemy who should be led out again into the night ? Have you any divination ? "

" I have no divination," said the Priest. " I cannot tell one thing or the other, nor each from the other in the case of this young man. But perhaps he is one of the Gods seeking shelter among men, or perhaps he is a fancy thing, warlock, but not doing evil. Or perhaps he is from the demons ; or perhaps he is a man like ourselves, and seeking shelter during some long wandering."

When the Chief heard this he asked the Pilot, not as a man possessing divine knowledge, but as one who had travelled and knew the sea, whether he knew this Stranger and whence he came. To which the Pilot answered :

" Captain, I do not know this young man nor whence he comes, nor any of his tribe, nor have I

The Missioner

seen any like him save once three slaves who stood
in a market-place of the Romans in a town that was
subject to a great lord who was a Frank and not a
Breton, and who was hated by the people of his town
so that later they slew him. Then these three slaves
were loosened, and they came to the house of the
Priest of the Gods of that country, and they told me
the name of the people whence they sprang. But I
have forgotten it. Only I know that it is among the
vineyard lands. There the day and the night are
equally divided all the year long, and if the snow
falls it falls gently and for a very little while, and
there are all manner of birds, and those people are
very rich, and they have great houses of stone. Now
I believe this Stranger to be a man like ourselves,
born of a woman, and coming northward upon some
purpose which we do not know. It may be for
merchandise, or it may be for the love of singing
and of telling stories to men."

When he had said this they all looked at the
Stranger and they saw that he had with him a little
instrument that was not known to them, for it
was a flute of metal. It was of silver, as they could
see, long drawn and very delicately made, and with
this had he summoned at the gate.

The Chief then brought out with his own hands a
carven chair, on which he seated the Stranger, and
he put into his right hand a gold cup taken from
the Romans in a city of the Franks, upon which was
faintly carved a cross, and round the rim of which

On Everything

were four precious stones, an emerald, a ruby, an
amethyst, and a diamond; and going to a skin
which he had taken in a Gascon raid, he poured out
wine into that chalice and went down upon one
knee as is proper to strangers when they are to be
entertained, and put a cloth over his arms and bade
him drink. But when the young man saw the cross
faintly carved upon the cup and the four precious
stones at the corners of it, he shuddered a little and
put it aside as though it were a sacred thing, at
which they all marvelled. Yet he longed for the
wine. And they, understanding that in some way
this ornament was sacred to his Gods, gently took it
from him and through courtesy put it aside upon a
separate place which was reserved for honourable
vessels, and poured him other wine into a wooden
stoop; and this he drank, holding it out now to one
and now to another, but last and chiefly to their
Captain; and as he drank it he drank it with signs
of amity.

Then by way of payment for so much kindness he
took his silver flute and blew upon it shrill notes, all
very sweet, and the sweeter for their choice and
distance one from another, until they listened,
listening every man with those beside him like one
man, for they had never heard such a sound; and as
he played one man saw one thing in his mind and
one another thing; for one man saw the long and
easy summer seas that roll after a prosperous boat
filled with spoil, whether of fishes or of booty, when

the square sail is taken aft by a warm wind in the summer season, and the high mountains of home first show beyond the line of the sea. And another man saw a little valley, narrow, with deep pasture, wherein he had been bred and had learned to plow the land with horses before ever he had come to the handling of a tiller or the bursting of water upon the bows. And another saw no distinct and certain thing, but vague and pleasurable hopes fulfilled, and the advent of great peace. And another saw those heights of the hills to which he ever desired to return.

But the old Pilot, straining with wonder in his eyes as the music rose, thought confusedly of all that he had seen and known; of the twirling tides upon the Breton coast and of the great stone towns, of the bright vestments of the ordered armies in the market-places and of the vineyard land.

When the Stranger had ceased so to play upon his instrument they applauded, as their custom was, by cries, some striking the armour upon the ground so that it rang, and by gesture and voice they begged him play again.

The second time he played all those men heard one thing: which was a dance of young men and women together in some country where there was little fear. The tune went softly, and was softly repeated, full of the lilt of feet, and when it was ended they knew that the dance was done.

This time they were so pleased that they waited

a little before they would applaud, but the old
Pilot, remembering more strongly than ever the
vineyard land, moved his right hand back and forward with delight as in some way he would play
music with it, and thus by a communication of heart
to heart stirred in that Stranger a new song; and
taking up his flute for the third time he blew upon
it a different strain, at which some were confused,
others hungry in their hearts, though they could
not have told you why, but the old Pilot saw great
and gracious figures moving over a land subject to
blessedness; he saw that in the faces of these
figures (which were those of the Immortals) stood
present at once a complete satisfaction and a joyous
energy and a solution of every ill. "These," he said
to himself in the last passion of the music, "these
are true Gods." But suddenly the music ceased,
and with it the vision also.

For the great pleasure which the Flute Player
had given them they desired to keep him in their
company, and so they did for three full years. That
is, the winter long, the seed time, and the time of
harvest; and the next harvest also, and another
harvest more, during which time he played them
many tunes, and learnt their tongue.

Now, his Gods were his own, but he pined for the
lack of their worship and for Priests of his own sort,
and when he would explain these in his own manner
some believed him, but some did not believe him.
And to those who believed him he brought a man

The Missioner

from the South, from beyond the Dovrefield, who
baptised them with water: as for those who would
not have this they looked on, and kept to their own
decree: but there was as yet no division among
them. A little while after the third harvest, hearing that the fleet, which was of twelve boats, would
make for Roman land, he begged to go with it, for
he was sick for his own, but first he made them take
an oath that they would molest none, nor even
barter with any, until they had landed him in his
own land. The Chief took this oath for them, and
though his oath was worth the oath of twelve
men, twelve other men swore with him. In this
way the oath was done. So they took the Flute
Player for three days over the sea before the
wind called Eager, which is the north-east wind,
and blows at the beginning of the open season; they
took him at the beginning of the fourth year since
his coming among them, and they landed him in
a little boat in a seaport of the Franks, on Roman
land. . . .

The Faith went over the world as very light seed
goes upon the wind, and no one knows the drift on
which it blew; it came to one place and to another,
and to each in a different way. It came, not to
many men, but always to one heart, till all men had
hold of it.

The Dream ◇ ◇ ◇ ◇ ◇

THE experience I am about to set down was perhaps the result, and at any rate it was the
sequel, of a conversation engaged between three
men in London in the year 1903.

Of these three men one was returned but recently
from South Africa, where he had seen all too much
of the war; another was a kindly, wealthy, sober sort
of man, young, virtuous, and full of inquiry; the third
was a hack.

It was about the season of Easter and of spring,
when actually and physically one can feel and handle
the force of life about one, all ready to break
bounds; but these young men (for no one of
them was yet of middle age) preferred to talk
of things more shadowy and less certain than
the air and the life and the English spring all
around. Things more shadowy and less certain,
but to the mind of youth, being a vigorous mind
things fixed and absorbing; destiny, for instance,
and the nature of man.

Not one of these three, however, affirmed in this
conversation (which I so well remember!) any
definite scheme. They spoke in terms of violent
opinion, of argument, and of analogy, but none of
the three came forward with a faith or even with

The Dream

a philosophy from which one felt he could not be
shaken. The more remarkable was it, therefore,
that one of them on his return in the early morning
to his rooms, after this young and long conversation
of a mixed sort, such as men entering upon life will
often indulge, should have suffered and should have
remembered an exact and even terrible vision. It
would indeed be inexplicable that he should have
suffered such a thing as a consequence of his waking
thoughts, though, if there be influences upon minds
other than the influences they themselves can bring
—if there be influences from without, and other wills
determining our dreams—then what next followed
is less difficult to comprehend. For, when he had
fallen asleep, it seemed to him at once that he was
in the midst of a very gay and pleasant company in
a sort of palace whereof the vast room in which
he stood was one out of very many that opened one
into the other in sequence. The crowd, and he with
it, went forward slowly towards a banquet which he
heard was prepared. He did not see among those
he spoke to, and who spoke to him, any face with
which he was familiar or to which he could attach a
name; and yet he seemed to know them all, in that
curious inconsequence of dreams, and one in especial,
at some distance from him, which seemed to have
been lost once, and now to be seen again through
the crowd, was a face the sight of which moved in
him a very passionate memory: yet it was no early
memory.

On Everything

So they went forward, and soon they were all
seated at a table of enormous length, so long that
its length seemed to have some purpose about it;
and at the farther end of this table was a door leading out of that hall. It was a door not very large
for so magnificent a space; such a door as a man or
woman could easily open with a common gesture,
and pass through and shut behind them quickly.

Now, for the first time, when they were eating
and drinking, it seemed to him that the conversation took on meaning, and a more consecutive
meaning than is usual in dreams; when, just as that
new phase of his dream had begun, one of the
guests, a little to the left of the place opposite to
him, a woman of middle age who had been somewhat silent, rose without apology, and without warning left her place he hardly knew how, and passed
out of the room through the door that he had
noticed. It shut behind her. No one mentioned
or noticed her going, but in a little while another
and another had risen and had gone. And still as
each guest departed, some in the midst of a sen-
tence, some during a silence in the talk, there increased upon him an appalling sense of unusual
things; it was appalling to him that no one said
good-bye, that none of the fellows of those who
so departed turned to them or noticed their going,
and that none of those who so departed returned
or made any promise to return. Next he noticed
with an increasing ill-ease, by some inconsequence

of his dream, that when he watched the departure of a guest (as the others did not) he saw
the empty chair and the gap left in the ranks;
but when he looked again after speaking to some
other to the right or left the gap was somehow less
defined, and when he looked yet again it was no
longer to be noticed or perceived; though it could
not be said that the chair was filled or was removed,
but in some way the absence of the man or woman
who had been there ceased to be marked, and it was
as though they had never been present at all. It
was not often that he cared to look for more than a
moment at one or another of these risings from the
feast; yet in the moment's observation he could see
very different things. Some rose as though in terror;
some as though in weariness; some startled, as at a
sudden command which they alone could hear; some
in a natural manner as though at an appointed
moment. But there was no order or method in
their going: only all went through that door.

His mind was now oppressed by the change which
comes in dreams, and turns them sometimes from
phantasy to horror. There sat opposite him a man
somewhat older than himself, with a face vigorous
and yet despairing, not without energy, and trained
in self-command. And this man answered his thoughts
at once, as thoughts are answered in dreams. He
said that it was of no use wondering why any guest
left that feast, nor what there was, if there was
anything, beyond the door through which this in-

consequential passage was made. Even as he was saying this he himself, suddenly looking towards it with an expression of extreme sadness and abandon-ment, rose abruptly, bowed to no one, and went out. At his departure the dreamer heard a little sigh, and he who had sighed said that doors of their nature led from one place to another, and then he tittered a little as though he had said a clever thing. Then another, a large happy man, laughed somewhat too loudly, and said that only fools discussed what none could know. A third, still upon that same theme, said in fixed, contented manner, that, in the nature of things, nothing was beyond the door. At which, the first who had spoken tittered again, and said doors of their nature led somewhere. Even as he said it his eyes filled with tears, and he also rose and went out.

For the first time during this increasing pressure of mystery and disaster (for so the dreamer felt it) he watched the figure of that guest; none of his companions about him dared or chose to do so; but the dreamer fixedly watched, and he saw the figure going down the long perspective of the hall very rapidly and very directly. It did not hesitate nor look back for one moment, it passed through—it was gone.

The dreamer suddenly felt the wine of that feast, the words spoken round him, more full of meaning and of novelty; the noise of speech, though more confused, was more pleasing and louder; the candles were far more bright. He had forgotten, or was just

The Dream

forgetting, all that other mood of his dream, when it seemed to him that in a sense all that converse was struck dumb. He heard no sound; he was cut off. Their hands still moved, their eyes and lips framed words and repeated glances, but around him, and for him, there was silence. The candles burned bright through the length of the room, and brightest, as in a guiding manner, towards the end of it where was the Door. He felt a thrill pass from his face. He rose and walked directly—no one speaking to him or noticing him at all—down the long, narrow space behind their chairs. It took him but a moment, innumerable as were those whom he must pass. His hand was upon the latch; with his head bent forward somewhat, and downwards, in the attitude of a man hurrying, he passed through. And, not knowing what he did, but doing it as though by habit, he shut the door between him and the feast, and immediately he was in a complete and utterly silent darkness. But he still was.

The Silence of the Battlefields 〜 〜

WHOEVER has had occasion, whether for study or for curiosity, to visit many of the battlefields of Europe, must have been especially struck by their silence. There are many things combining to produce this impression, but when all have been accounted for, something over remains. Thus it is true that in any countryside the contrast between the noise of the great fight that fills one's mind and the natural calm of woods and of fields must penetrate the mind ; and, again, it is evident that any piece of land which one closely examines, noting all its details for the purposes of history, must seem more lonely and deserted than those general views in which the eye comprehends so much of the work of man ; because all this special watching of particular corners, noting of ranges and the rest, make one's progress slow, keep one's eyes close fixed to things more or less near, and thus allow one to appreciate how far between men are save in the towns. But there is more than this. It can be proved that there is more. For the same sense of complete loneliness does not take a man in other similar work. He does not feel it when he is surveying for a map nor when he is searching for an historic site other than that of battle. But the battlefields are lonely.

The Silence of the Battlefields

Some few, especially in this crowded island, are not lonely. Life has overtaken them, spreading outwards from the towns. By what a curious irony, for instance, the racecourse at Lewes, with a shouting throng of men as the horses go by, corresponds precisely to the place where must have been the thickest of the advance on Montfort's right as he led them to attack the King. Evesham is not lonely. Battle is full of houses and of villas, and the chief centre of the fight is in a garden.

But for the most part the great battlefields are lonely; and their loneliness is unnatural and oppressive. In some way they repel men. Trasimene is the lonely shore of a marsh. One would imagine that a place so famous would be in some way visited. One of the great sewers of cosmopolitan travel runs close by; one would imagine that the historic interest of the place would bring men from that railway to the shore upon which so very nearly the Orientals destroyed us. There is no such publicity. Sitting at evening near those reeds, where the great fight was fought, one has a feeling, rare in Italy, commoner in the north, of complete isolation. There is nothing but water and the evening sky, and it is so mournful that one might imagine it a place to which things doomed would come to die.

Roncesvalles, which means so little in the military history of Europe and so much in her literature, is a profound gorge, cleft right into the earth 3000 feet, and clothed with such mighty beech woods that for these alone, apart from its history, one might imagine it to be perpetually visited. It is not visited. No house is near it, save the huddled huts round the gloomy place of pilgrimage upon the farther side of the pass. A silence more profound, a sense of recession more complete, is not to be discovered upon any of the great roads of Europe—for one of the great roads goes by the place where Roland died, but very few travel along it.

Toulouse is popular and noisy; surrounded by so many small market gardens and so busy and humming a Southern life (detestable to quiet men!) that you might think no site near it was touched with loneliness. But there is such a site. It is the crest beyond the city where Wellington's victory was won. More curious still, Waterloo, at the very gates of Brussels, within a stone's throw, one may say, of building sites for suburbs, is the only lonely place in its neighbourhood. That valley, or rather that little dip which is so great in military history and yet which did so little to change the general movement of the world, is the one deserted set of fields that you can find for a long way round. And the soil of Belgium, a gridiron of railways, stuffed with industry, a place where one short walk takes you from a town to a town anywhere throughout the little State, is still remarkable for the way in which its battlefields seem to fend off the presence of man. The plateau of Fleurus, the marshy banks of Jemappes, the roll of Neerwinden, all illustrate what I mean.

If one considers in what two places since Christendom was Christendom most was done to save Christendom from destruction, one will fix upon the Catalaunian Fields and upon that low tableland in the fork of the two rivers between Poitiers and Tours. In the first Attila was broken, Asia from the East; in the second the Mohammedan, Asia from the South. The Catalaunian Fields have a bleakness amazing to the traveller. Nothing perhaps so near so much wealth is so utterly alone. Great folds of empty land that will grow little, that only lately were planted with stunted pine trees that they might at least grow something, weary the eye. One dead straight road, Roman in origin, Gallic in its continuance, drives right across the waste. It is there that the Huns were broken. It is from that point that their sullen retreat eastward was permitted, as was permitted in 1792 the retreat eastward of the Royal Armies from their check in that same plain at Valmy; and Valmy also is intensely lonely, a bare ridge despoiled to-day even of its mill, and the little chapel raised to the soul of Kellerman hides itself away so that you do not see it until you are close upon the place.

Poitiers has the same loneliness. The Mohammedan had ridden up from the Pyrenees, ricochetted from the walls of Toulouse, but poured on like a flood into the centre of Gaul. Charles the Hammer broke him in the fields beyond Vouneuil. The district is populous and the Valley of the Clain is full of pastures and among the tenderest of European valleys, but as you drift down stream and approach this place the plateau upon the right above you grows bare, and it was there, so far as modern scholarship can be certain, that the last effort of the Arabs was forced back.

That other battle of Poitiers among the vineyards, the Black Prince's battle, one would imagine, could not seem lonely, for it was fought in the midst of tilled land full of vineyards and right above the great high road which leads south-east from the town. But lonely it is, and if you will go up the little gully where the head of the French column advanced against the English archers upon the high land above, you will not find a man to tell you the memories of the place.

Creçy was fought close to a county town; but the same trick of landscape or of influence is also played there. The town hides itself in a little hollow upon the farther flank of a hill, and though the right of Edward's line reposed upon it, and though it was within a bowshot of the houses that the boy his son was pressed so hard, yet Creçy hides away from the battlefield. And as you come in by the eastern road, which takes you all along the crest of the English position, there is nothing before you but a naked and

The Silence of the Battlefields

a silent land, falling in a dip to where the first of
the French charge failed, and rising in long empty
lengths of fallow and of grass to where you can see,
a single mark for the eye in so much loneliness, the
rude cross standing on the place where the blind
King of Bohemia fell.

Loneliest of all, with a loneliness which perpetually haunts me whenever I write of it, is that battlefield which I know best and have most closely studied.
It is the battlefield on which, as I believe, more was
done to affect both military and general history than
on any other—the battlefield of Wattignies. Here
the Revolution certainly stood, to go under with the
fall of Maubeuge, which was at the last gasp for
food, or, with the raising of that siege, to go forward.
By the success at Wattignies the siege was raised.
In military history also it is of great account, for at
Wattignies for the first time the great mind of
Carnot, the darting, aquiline mind of that man whose
school of tactics produced Napoleon, first dealt with
an army. At Wattignies for the first time the concentration at the fullest expense of fatigue, of overwhelming force upon one point of the objective,
came into play and was successful. Such tactics
needed the Infantry which as a fact were used in
their development. Still, they were new. Now,
Wattignies, where so much was done to change the
art of war and to transform Europe, is as lonely as
anything on earth. Lines of high trees, a wood
almost uncultivated (a rare thing in France), a swept,

wintry upland without a house or a barn, a little
huddled group of poor steadings round a tiny church,
and against it all the while rain and hard weather
driving from the French plains below: that is Wattignies. Up through those sunken ways by which
Duquesnoy's division charged you will not meet a
single human being, and that heath over which the
emigrant nobles countercharged for the last time
under the white flag is similarly bereft of men.
Nowhere do you more feel the unnatural loneliness
of those haunted places of honour than in this which
I believe to be the chief one of all the European
fields.

Novissima Hora   ❧   ❧   ❧   ❧

TIME, which is to the mind a function of the mind, stretches and contracts, as all men know, when the mind impelled by forces not its own demands the expansion or the lessening of time. Thus in a moment, as the foolish physicists can prove, long experiences of dreams are held; and thus hours upon hours of other men's lives are lost to us for ever when we lie in profound sleep; and I knew a man who, sleeping through a morning upon the grassy side of a hill many years ago, slept through news that seemed to have ruined him and his, and slept on to a later moment when the news proved false and the threat of disaster was lifted; during those hours of agony there had been for him no time.

They say that with men approaching dissolution some trick of time is played, or at least that when death is very near indeed the whole scale and structure of thought changes, just as some have imagined (and it is a reasonable suspicion) that the common laws governing matter do not apply to it in some last stage of tenuity, so the ordered sequence of the mind takes on something fantastic and moves during such moments in a void.

On Everything

So must it have been with that which I will now describe.

A man lay upon a bed of a common sort in a room which was bare of ornament. But he had forgotten the room. He was a man of middle age, corpulent, and one whose flesh and the skin of whose flesh had sagged under disease. His eyes were closed, his mouth, which was very fine, delicate, and firm, alone of his features preserved its rigour. Those features had been square and massive, their squareness and their strength the more emphasised by the high forehead with its one wisp of hair. But though the strength of character remained behind the face, the muscular strength had left it, for that body had suffered agony.

The man so lying was conscious of little; the external world was already beyond his reach. He knew that somehow he was not suffering pain, and the mortal fatigue that oppressed him had, in that unexpected absence of pain, some opportunity for repose. Neither his room nor what was left of companionship round him, nor the voices that he knew and loved, nor those others that he knew too well and despised, reached his senses. For many years the air in which he had lived and in which he was now perishing had been to him in his captivity a mournful delight. It was a tropical air, but enlivened by the freshness of the sea and continually impelled in great sea winds above him. Now he felt that air no longer, and might have

been so many thousand miles away in the place
where he had been born, or many thousand miles
more, in the snows of a great campaign, or under
the violent desert sun of certain remembered battles;
it was all one to him, for he only held to life by one
thread within, and outer things had already left him.

Within, however, his mind in that last weakness
still busily turned; no longer considering as it had
considered during the activity of a marvellous life
what answers the great questions propounded to
the soul of man should receive, still less noting
practical and immediate needs or considering set
problems. His mind for once, almost for the first
time, was this last time seeing things go by.

First he saw dull pageantries which had been the
common stuff of his life, and he was confused by
half-remembered, half-restored, faint cheers of distant crowds, colours, and gold, and the twin flashes
of gems and of steel. And through it now and then
strains of solemn music, and now and then the tear-
ing cry of bronze : the bugles. All these sensations,
confused and blurred, re-arose, and as they re-arose,
welling up into him like a mist, there re-arose those
permanent concomitants of such things. He felt
again the nervous dread of folly and mishap, wondered upon the correctness of his conduct, whether
he had not given offence somewhere to someone . . .
whether he had not been the subject of criticism by
some tongue he feared. And as all that part of his
great life returned to him, his face even in that

extremity showed some faint traces of concern such
as it had borne when in truth and in the body he
had moved in the midst of a Court.

Next, like shadows disappearing, all that ghostly
hubbub passed, but before he could be alone another
picture succeeded, and he thought to feel beneath
him the rolling of the sea. He was a young man
looking for land, with others standing behind upon
the deck, watching him in envy because of the
miracles he was to do with armed men when he
should touch the shore. And yet he was not a young
man. He was a man already weighted with dis-
appointment and with loss of love, and with some
confused conception of breaking under an immense
strain ; and those who were on the deck behind him
watching him, watched him with awe and with pity,
and with a sort of dread that did not relieve his
spirit. So young and old in the same moment, he
felt in the brain the swinging of a ship's deck. So
he strained for land, a land where he should con-
quer, and at the same time it was a land where he
should be utterly alone, and utterly forget, and be
filled with nothing but defeat. The contradiction
held him altogether.

Then this movement also steadied and changed,
and he had the sensation of a man walking up some
steep hill, some hill too steep. He was leading a
horse and the horse stumbled. It was bitterly cold,
but he did not feel the cold : the roaring and the
driving round him in the snow. Next he was in the

Novissima Hora

saddle; there was a little eminence from which he saw a plain. Slight as the beast was his seat galled him. He sat his mount badly, and he dreaded lest it should start with him as it had started the day before. But even as he so worried himself on his bad horsemanship, all his mind changed at quite another sight.

For in the plain below that little height the great battalions went forward, rank upon rank upon rank; it was a review and it was a battle and it was a campaign. Mad imagery! the uniforms were the uniforms of gala, the drum-majors went before the companies of the Guard, gigantic, twirling their gigantic staves; the lifted trumpets of the Cuirassiers sounded as though upon some great stage, for the mere glory of the sound. And mass upon mass, regular, instinct with purpose, innumerable, the army passed below. There was no end to it. He knew, he was certain, as he strained his eyes, that it would never end. It was afoot, and it would march for ever. Far off, beyond the line, upon the flank of it, distant and terrible went the packed mass of the guns, and you could hear faintly amid the other noises of the advance the clatter-clank-clank of the limber. And from so far off he saw the leading sabres of commanders saluting him from his old arm. Here again was a mixture for him of things that do not mix in the true world: Glory and Despair. This endless army was his, and yet would go on beyond him. It was his and not his. There was room upon the colours for a million names of victories, but every victory in some way carried the stamp of defeat. And yet seeing all that pageant as the precursor of failure, he saw it also as something constructive. He thought of wood that burns and is consumed, but is the fuel of a flame of fire and all that fire can do.

As he so thought, like a wind and a spirit blowing through the whole came some vast conception of a a God. And once again the mixed, the dual feeling seized him, more greatly than before. It was a God that drove them all, and him. And that God was in his childhood, and he remembered his childhood very clearly. It was something of which he had been convinced in childhood, a security of good. . . . Look how the army moved ! . . .

And now it had halted.

Here his mind failed, and he had died. It was Napoleon.

On Rest ∽　∽　∽　∽　∽　∽

THERE was a priest once who preached a sermon
to the text of "Abba, Father." On that text
one might preach anything, but the matter that he
chose was "Rest." He was not yet in middle age,
and those who heard him were not yet even young.
They could not understand at all the moment of his
ardent speech, and even the older men, seeing him
to be but in the central part of life, wondered that
he should speak so. His eyes were illuminated by
the vision of something distant; his heart was not ill
at ease, but, as it were, fixedly expectant, and he
preached from his little pulpit in that little chapel of
the Downs, with rising and deeper powers of the
voice, so that he shook the air; yet all this energy
was but the praise or the demand for the surcease
of energy, and all this sound was but the demand for
silence.

It is a thing, I say, incomprehensible to the young,
but gradually comprehended as the years go droning
by, that in all things (and in proportion to the intensity of the life of each) there comes this appetite for
dissolution and for repose: I do not mean that repose beyond which further effort is demanded, but
something final and supreme.

On Everything

This priest, a year or so after he had appealed
with his sermon before that little country audience
in the emptiness of the Downs, died. He had that
which he desired, Rest. But what is it? What is
the nature of this thing?

Note you how great soldiers, when their long campaigns are done, are indifferent to further wars, and
look largely upon the nature of fighting men, their
objects, their failures, their victories, their rallying,
their momentary cheers. Not that they grow indifferent to that great trade which is the chief business of a State, the defence or the extension of the
common weal; but that after so much expense of all
the senses our God gave them, a sort of charity and
justice fills their minds. I have often remarked how
men who had most lost and won, even in arms, would
turn the leisured part of their lives to the study of
the details of struggle, and seemed equally content
to be describing the noble fortunes of an army,
whether it were upon the crest of advancing victory,
or in the agony of a surrender. This was because
the writers had found Rest. And throughout the
history of Letters—of Civilisation, and of contemporary friends, one may say that in proportion to the
largeness of their action is this largeness and security
of vision at the end.

Now, note another thing: that, when we speak of
an end, by that very word we mean two things.
For first we mean the cessation of Form, and perhaps
of Idea; but also we mean a goal, or object, to which

the Form and the Idea perpetually tended, without which they would have had neither meaning nor existence, and in which they were at last fulfilled. Aristotle could give no summing up but this to all his philosophy, that there was a nature, not only of all, but of each, and that the end determined what that nature might be; which is also what we Christians mean when we say that God made the world; and great Rabelais, when his great books were ending, could but conclude that all things tended to their end. Tennyson also, before he died, having written for so many years a poetry which one must be excused in believing considerable, felt, as how many have felt it, the thrumming of the ebb tide when the sea calls back the feudal allegiance of the rivers. I know it upon Arun bar. The Flood, when the sea heaves up and pours itself into the inland channels, bears itself creatively, and is like the manhood of a man—first tentative, then gathering itself for action, then sweeping suddenly at the charge. It carries with it the wind from the open horizon, it determines suddenly, it spurs, and sweeps, and is victorious; the current races; the harbour is immediately full.

But the ebb tide is of another kind. With a long, slow power, whose motive is at once downward steadily towards its authority and its obedience and desire, it pushes as with shoulders, home; and for many hours the stream goes darkly, swiftly, and steadily. It is intent, direct, and level. It

On Everything

is a thing for evenings, and it is under an evening
when there is little wind, that you may best observe
the symbol thus presented by material things. For
everything in nature has in it something sacramental,
teaching the soul of man ; and nothing more possesses
that high quality than the motion of a river when it
meets the sea. The water at last hangs dully, the
work is done ; and those who have permitted the
lesson to instruct their minds are aware of consum-
mation.

Men living in cities have often wondered how it
was that the men in the open who knew horses and
the earth or ships and the salt water risk so much—
and for what reward ? It is an error in the very
question they ask, rather than in the logical puzzle
they approach, which falsifies their wonder. There
is no reward. To die in battle, to break one's neck
at a hedge, to sink or to be swamped are not
rewards. But action demands an end ; there is a
fruit to things ; and everything we do (here at least,
and within the bonds of time) may not exceed the
little limits of a nature which it neither made nor
acquired for itself, but was granted.

Some say that old men fear death. It is the theme
of the debased and the vulgar. It is not true.
Those who have imperfectly served are ready enough;
those who have served more perfectly are glad—as
though there stood before them a natural transition
and a condition of their being.

So it says in a book "all good endings are but

shining transitions." And, again, there is a sonnet
which says :

> We will not whisper : we have found the place
> Of silence and the ancient halls of sleep,
> And that which breathes alone throughout the deep
> The end and the beginning ; and the face
> Between the level brows of whose blind eyes
> Lie plenary contentment, full surcease
> Of violence, and the ultimate great peace
> Wherein we lose our human lullabies.
>
> Look up and tell the immeasurable height
> Between the vault of the world and your dear head ;
> That's Death, my little sister, and the Night
> That was our Mother beckons us to bed :
> Where large oblivion in her house is laid
> For us tired children now our games are played.

Indeed, one might quote the poets (who are the
teachers of mankind) indefinitely in this regard.
They are all agreed. What did Sleep and Death to
the body of Sarpedon? They took it home. And
every one who dies in all the Epics is better for the
dying. Some complain of it afterwards I will admit ;
but they are hard to please. Roland took it as the
end of battle ; and there was a Scandinavian fellow
caught on the north-east coast, I think, who in dying
thanked God for all the joy he had had in his life—
as you may have heard before. And St. Anthony
of Assisi (not of Padua) said, " Welcome, little sister
Death ! " as was his way. And one who stands right
up above most men who write or speak said it was

the only port after the tide-streams and bar-handling
of this journey.

So it is; let us be off to the hills. The silence
and the immensity that inhabit them are the simul-
acra of such things.